Confrontinfort

Confronting Our Discomfort

Clearing the Way for Anti-Bias
in Early Childhood

Tamar Jacobson

Foreword by Mem Fox

HEINEMANN
Portsmouth, NH

Heinemann
A division of Reed Elsevier Inc.
361 Hanover Street
Portsmouth, NH 03801–3912
www.heinemann.com

Offices and agents throughout the world

The author and publisher wish to thank those who have generously given permission to reprint borrowed material:

"America" by Marquis Woolford is used by permission of the poet.

Excerpt of "In and Out of Confidence" by Tamar Meyer from the *Association of Young Children of Western New York Newsletter*, November/December 1998. Reprinted by permission of AEYC of WNY.

"Everybody's Paid But Teacher" by J. H. Harris in *Everybody's Paid But the Teacher* by Patricia A. Carter. Reprinted by permission of Teachers College Press.

Library of Congress Cataloging-in-Publication Data
Jacobson, Tamar.
  Confronting our discomfort : clearing the way for anti-bias in early childhood / Tamar Jacobson.
    p. cm.
  Includes bibliographical references.
  ISBN 0-325-00569-9 (alk. paper)
    1. Multicultural education—United States.   2. Discrimination in education—United States.   3. Early childhood education—Social aspects—United States.
4. Early childhood teachers—United States—Attitudes.   I. Title.

LC1099.J33 2003
370.117—dc21   2003011647

Editor: Danny Miller
Production service: Denise Botelho
Production coordination: Vicki Kasabian
Cover design: Catherine Hawkes, Cat & Mouse
Typesetter: House of Equations, Inc.
Manufacturing: Steve Bernier

Printed in the United States of America on acid-free paper
07 06 05 04 03 VP 1 2 3 4 5

I dedicate this book to my dear friend,

Charles Haynie

Shalom Lecha Chaver

(Goodbye/go in peace, my friend)

"The fight for equality and justice is important in and of itself,
because it is right, not because it can guarantee us
a pain-free, perfect, brave new world."
Phyllis Chesler, *Woman's Inhumanity to Woman*

Contents

Foreword

Society is created through the experiences of children who grow up. This book is a case in point.

Tamar Jacobson grew up Jewish in the racist African country then known as Rhodesia, now called Zimbabwe. At school she met my sister Jan, became her best friend, and through Jan met my nonracist missionary mother who, she claims—with glorious extravagance—changed her life. In our house Tamar saw for the first time a print of the Madonna and Child in which the mother and the child had brown skins, not white. It was the beginning, for her, of a new direction along life's way.

This book is a major destination on that journey. Those who read it will be able to follow in her footsteps, grateful for her unique guidance along the tricky path toward an anti-bias curriculum for educators of young children.

Reading *Confronting Our Discomfort* is not always a comfortable trek since Tamar Jacobson forces us to see our own shortcomings and biases at the very same time as we smugly judge others for theirs. We move from comfort to discomfort, and back again, challenged by her disquiet, moved by her perspective, and changed by her ideas.

She and I know, after a lifetime of working with children under five, that everything important in society is built upon the experiences of its young children. We know that inequality, unemployment, hunger, abuse, illiteracy, and bias will often lead to more of the same in adulthood unless early intervention occurs. The hope of children, their light along the way, their ticket to a better future lies in the hands of their early educators who have an awesome choice: to perpetuate the negatives in children's lives or to eradicate them.

Confronting Our Discomfort teaches us how to eradicate bias. We discover in these pages how we learned our own biases from adults who were, above all, our protectors. We had to believe what they told us since our belief in their biases was a safety device for getting on in the world in which we grew up. It was a survival strategy. But it was our survival alone, and we ignored the implications for those around us.

In this book, Tamar Jacobson wakes us up and shows us how to address our own biases so we can teach an anti-bias curriculum with a clearer conscience and a greater understanding of society and its inequalities. In other words, she shows us how to change the world.

Mem Fox

Acknowledgments

There have been all kinds of influences along the way that have made an impact on my attitudes and beliefs about bias and young children. This book is the result of self-reflection about my personal and professional life and how it has affected my teaching. I am grateful to everyone who has traveled with me on my anti-bias journey for without them I would not be able to share my stories with you.

Special thanks to my beautiful, creative and loving son, Gilad, who has from the instant of his birth taught me about unconditional love and human relationships, and who has born the brunt of so many of my unconscious mistakes as a parent; my husband, Tom, my best friend, who gives me the love, encouragement, and support to be myself professionally and personally; Zehava Winter, supervisor from the Israeli Ministry of Education, who taught me about integrity and professionalism; and the staff of the University at Buffalo Child Care Center, who took me into their "home" in 1993. I admire you for your model interactions of respect, and the excellence of care and education you provide for each and every child.

Thank you to the many people who have strengthened my courage, awareness, and perseverance in the work that I do: Susan Koehler, Lisa Stefanie, Susan Schwartz, Tom Frantz, Steve Brown, Charles Haynie, and Judy Duchan. For the safe space you gave me to reflect on my life's journey, I thank Inge Wallerstein, Nan Partridge, "Nanny" Margaret, Jan Delacourt, Ziva Levita, and "Bob."

I give thanks to people I have heard or read, and who opened, reinforced, and inspired me—too many to mention, perhaps, so these names will have to suffice: Bruce Perry, Lilian Katz, Bill Ayers, Janet Gonzalez-Mena, Louise Derman-Sparks, Germaine Greer, bell hooks, Jonathan Kozol, Alfie Kohn, and Marian Wright Edelman.

My deepest gratitude goes to all the women of the Anti-Bias Support-Supervision Group. With great courage, they opened themselves up and dared to confront their personal biases. Even with discomfort on that hot seat, they readily shared their emotions with me, fellow group members, and now the reader.

Thanks, Mom, for the gift of a typewriter on my sixteenth birthday. Back then you gave me the tools to find my voice, even as I am sure you dreamed of doing for yourself had you only felt deserving enough to try. I am especially grateful to my brother, Norman, for his relentless pursuit of justice for humanity through his scholarly works. His voice accompanies me every day in the way I think politically and ideologically.

And finally, my editor Danny Miller, who I like to think has become an important friend, and without whom this book would simply not have happened. Danny, I needed someone to endorse me as a valuable person—thank you.

Confronting Our Discomfort

What We Do Matters

The fundamental message of the teacher is this:
You can change your life. Whoever you are, wherever
you've been, whatever you've done, the teacher invites
you to a second chance, another round, perhaps a
different conclusion. . . . To teach consciously for social
justice, to teach for social change, adds a complicating
element to that fundamental message, making it more
layered, more dense, more excruciatingly difficult to
enact, and at the same time sturdier, more engaging,
more powerful and joyful much of the time. . . . And so
the fundamental message of the teacher for social justice
is: You can change the world.

William Ayers, *Teaching for Social Justice*

Intolerance Matters

I have heard people say, time and again, that they have no prejudices
and that everyone is the same to them. In fact, some state that they
never even notice the color of a person's skin. They believe they are
unbiased. Most people have developed a color-blind approach where
not noticing the differences means being without prejudice. Sharon
Henry describes how the statement "I don't see color when I look at
children" makes her experience "a rush of discomfort and rage upon
hearing it":

> From my perspective, the "color-blind" belief diminishes me (re-
> gardless the intent of the speaker) and is not good for children
> of any culture. I am a cultural being and color-blind perspective
> denies that to me because it invariably reflects the belief that "we
> are all the same." My color is relevant to my experience as an
> African American woman in a racist society that uses skin color

as a determinant of who is and who isn't entitled to power and privilege. Moreover, my community knows it is vital to our children's health to resist put-downs based on skin color. . . . The color of our skin is not something to be ignored, but something to be celebrated by paying attention to and describing it. A color-blind position denies this reality. (Cronin, Derman-Sparks, Henry, Olatunji, and York 1998, 67)

Not seeing differences is a way to avoid facing any uncomfortable feelings that bias might raise within us. A child calls out: "Look Mom, he's in a wheelchair!" Mom (or her teacher) often replies quickly: "Shh. That's not nice!" Let's pause here and ask: What is not nice? The wheelchair? Noticing it? Pointing at it? Do we think the man in the wheelchair is unaware of being in it? Do we think much about any of these questions? Instead, a feeling of discomfort rises in us, unconsciously, and we try to avoid it as quickly as we can. Then we set up a wall to shut that feeling out, without realizing that, as the curious child is now silenced, so is our friend in the wheelchair. He becomes invisible with his life story, feelings, and identity. The child learns that there is something uncomfortable, almost dangerous, about noticing someone in a wheelchair and that she should not ask questions about it. The color-blind approach uses silence and avoidance and all are affected by it. All slip away into a silent consciousness and become invisible.

The primary objective of this book is to help teachers learn how to look at what stands in their own way as they try to implement anti-bias values in their classrooms. One of the obstacles is ourselves. With all of our discomfort zones, we stand in our own way of developing tolerance of diversity. Teachers struggle constantly to do the right thing and teach acceptance of diversity, but they become confused and frustrated when they understand a concept but feel, somehow, something is lacking. When I present and consult throughout the country, I hear time and again similar questions and concerns from teachers and teacher educators: What is an anti-bias curriculum? What is the difference between anti-bias and multicultural curriculum? Should I or shouldn't I celebrate holidays? We do anti-bias in our program but I still think it's not quite right—what can I do better? Many teacher-educators are frustrated as they send student-teachers out to schools and classrooms, only to find cooperating teachers who say things like:

We don't need to talk about differences, everyone is the same in my classroom. These same teachers deal with multicultural issues through stereotypical images or celebration of holidays only.

Teachers and teacher-educators, for the most part, are genuinely concerned about racism and oppression. Even though it seems as simple as making changes in myself and then education for tolerance will be easy, it is not. Discomfort is difficult to face. We are constantly taught by society and the media to acquire instant comfort through drugs, coffee, food, shopping—you name it. We are seldom taught to hold still and face feelings that cause us anxiety or to feel uneasy. Many of these feelings rise up within us moment-to-moment when we take on the challenge of anti-bias work.

Confronting our discomfort should always accompany teachers as they implement anti-bias values or teach acceptance. Teachers and teacher-educators can use this book as they do anti-bias work. However, it is not intended as a self-help book with solutions in terms of "follow steps one through six to redemption and the elimination of racism and intolerance." Instead, I describe feelings of discomfort; invite you, teachers and teacher-educators, to open up your minds and hearts with me, as we struggle to understand the complexity and nature of our own personal biases. In fact, we are unable to authentically teach about acceptance without engaging in reflection about ourselves.

Awareness Is Important

Right now, from my shelf, I take down nine books that talk about diversity and multicultural education. For example, Kendall's book, *Diversity in the Classroom: A Multicultural Approach to the Education of Young Children* (1983), describes child development, talks with parents about multicultural education, and gives specific, practical suggestions for what kinds of activities to use in the classroom. A short epilogue reminds us about institutional racism and how insidious it is. In the preface, the author states: "teachers' racial attitudes and a multicultural classroom environment—cannot be separated if our goal is positive, growth-producing education for all children" (xiii). In the first chapter the author goes on to say: "Teachers are models for children; therefore they should show respect and concern for all people. . . . Teachers pass their own values and attitudes on to children both intentionally and unintentionally; therefore it is important that they be keenly aware of their own attitudes and values," and *"A situation exists that encourages change in teachers' behavior without providing support for changes in attitudes. The result may be that teachers are sending children double messages"* (2–3) [italics mine].

McCracken writes in *Valuing Diversity: The Primary Years,* "Only through honest self-examination can we root out the prejudices that we have learned, practiced, and *intentionally or inadvertently passed on to children"* (1993, 8) [italics mine]. The remainder of McCracken's book gives suggestions to teachers about designing the physical environment and different teaching strategies, and even gives tips for appropriate field trips.

Each of the nine books is similar in its approach. They mention that teachers must self-examine or "root out prejudice." They remind teachers about institutional racism and laws that forbid segregation. They suggest what teachers might do in classrooms to teach young children about tolerance (Fu, Stremmel, and Treppte 1993, Neugebauer 1992, Ramsey 1998, Shapon-Shevin 1999, Vold 1992, York 1991). There is even a book that teaches teachers about disciplining children in a diverse society (Gordon and Browne 1996).

In *Multicultural Issues in Child Care,* Gonzalez-Mena (1993) describes the book as based on "cultural pluralism." Gonzalez-Mena reminds us that "we unconsciously teach the children whose lives we touch about ourselves through everything we do. . . . Consciously or not, we work to make the children we care for and teach into the kind of people who fit our culture" (xi). In this book, Gonzalez-Mena shares with the reader her own feelings of discomfort as she works with people from different cultures. She relates some of the discomfort to our wanting children to fit into what is familiar for us within our own culture.

Derman-Sparks writes an entire chapter devoted to "selfconsciousness raising activities" including encouraging teachers to form a support group if they intend to implement an anti-bias curriculum (Derman-Sparks 1989). In a later book, Derman-Sparks joins with Cronin, Henry, Olatunji, and York with a report from the Culturally Relevant Anti-Bias Leadership Project (1998). In this work, support combined with community activism is described through personal narrative experiences of the members of this important project. Participants describe their feelings of discomfort as they raise their consciousness (and, hopefully, ours—the readers) in their tireless efforts to end oppression.

The Discomfort

These are all excellent books and give teachers many different and wonderful ideas about what to do with children and how to talk with parents. They make a major contribution to the field of early childhood education and specifically education for acceptance of diversity. My work builds on these contributions and brings in another dimension for teachers and teacher-educators: our own discomfort. I add to their work that the process of becoming aware of bias is painful. The experts before me talk about our unconscious or "unintentional" behaviors with children. They emphasize the significance of becoming aware of the effects of institutional racism, white privilege, and the dominant culture on our attitudes. However, most books dealing with cultural tolerance do not deal with consciousness-raising specifically. As a teacher receiving all these instructions, what do I do with any discomfort I might be feeling? How do I "root out" my prejudice? Bias is uncomfortable. Many people do not believe they have prejudices. We cannot leave this aspect out when we ask teachers to change attitudes and behaviors.

By describing my own self-reflection in this book, I hope to show you that it is worthwhile to work through personal issues such as discomfort and pain. Indeed it has accompanied, enhanced, and strengthened my activist work with teachers, children, and families throughout my life. This approach is crucial in accompanying us, as we become effective facilitators of any anti-bias education. In fact, we are unable to authentically teach acceptance without self-reflection and confronting our discomfort. There are things we can do about it. You are not alone.

We Have Responsibilities and Opportunities

Typically, we think of teaching as being about teaching methods—not consciousness raising. Consider organizing support groups, self-awareness activities, journal writing, and other ways to come to terms or make peace with our discomfort as we work toward acceptance of diversity. We are constantly being told to celebrate diversity! How do we celebrate that which we fear? Childhood educators have a responsibility to face their discomfort. In fact, we perpetuate prejudice and racism by not doing that.

"There is no genetics in racism" (Perry 2001). Bruce Perry gives us research-based information about how the brain develops in the early years. By four-years-old the brain is 85 percent of its adult size. Perry's work reinforces that what we do, how we behave, and what we say really affects young children for the rest of their lives. More specifically, the way we treat young children affects how the brain develops. The greater opportunity children have to engage with diversity, the more they will learn to care about different people. Perry reminds us that human beings create language, religion, childrearing practices, family structure, cultural history, educational practices, arts, sciences, technology, and other beliefs. He assures us that it is not inevitable that we create societies that are violent. If we are responsible for creating all of our culture and beliefs as Perry suggests, surely we are able to change them just as well? It must just be a matter of acquiring the knowledge, becoming aware, and making a personal choice.

Many teachers are required to implement multicultural curriculum for young children. They are expected to relax their control on learned preconceived notions about how to behave, and what is expected, and to be open to everything without surprise. Teachers are expected to respect different ways of learning and parenting according to culture. Many authors suggest ways of doing this. Anti-bias education must display diversity but not stereotypically. Authentic anti-bias education includes diversity at every level: culture, ethnicity, gender, sexual orientation, special needs, and much more. It is very hard work, a challenge. It takes time, maybe forever.

In-depth anti-bias work means making a genuine and significant change in our own biased attitudes. How do we talk about differences, eliminate stereotypes, or become activists with children if we are uncomfortable with all these subjects—if we, ourselves, believe in some of the stereotypes we should be eliminating? It takes courage, and I suggest that you have compassion and respect for yourself as you take on this work. Eventually, we make peace with the idea that all of us are in some ways biased. By doing that we are able to negotiate with ourselves and determine which biases we choose to preserve and which we eliminate in ourselves. This type of self-reflection should be ongoing, accompanying us as we interact with children and families. In that way, we take responsibility for how we behave and the things we say.

Unconsciously Motivated Behaviors

Do we want to do unto others what we don't want them to do to us? For example, do we want to be humiliated or feel degraded? Do we enjoy people criticizing us or giving us empty praise? Do we enjoy punishment as opposed to support and guidance? Usually not! And yet we do these things to children without hesitation, often unconsciously. Many of us don't know where these reactions come from. I wonder if teachers feel that there is enough time for them to think about it very much. Once I was asked to write about children's resilience to inappropriate practices and named the article "What We Do Matters" (Jacobson 1999). I would think it was a trite thing to say and that people would wonder why I might write about this. After all, surely, wasn't it common knowledge that what we do to children affects them for the rest of their lives? And yet people were thrilled with the article and even asked me to do presentations and keynote speeches about it, as if the topic was new.

> Critical thinking, asking uncomfortable questions and taking risks are necessary skills for activism and taking a stand against bias. Martin Luther King Jr. said that the silence of good people is worse than bigoted acts. It is most difficult to take a stand against prejudice and injustice when one has been taught to obey and please those in power. Teachers have power with young children. They are capable of supporting children to think for themselves, ask difficult questions and take risks that challenge their decision-making abilities. On the other hand, they can teach young children to be helpless, fearful and unquestioning of obedience. (Jacobson 1999, 62)

Teachers are sent out into classrooms where they behave in ways and say things that affect children for the rest of their lives. The way in which we hand down our own biases will, in fact, affect children's perception of the world. We do have a choice about how we behave. We should be very concerned and passionate about the types of biases we might consciously or unconsciously hand down to children.

When we are unaware of our prejudice we react unconsciously in different ways. There are subtle things teachers do. For example, they might teach a unit on "sharing" but are unable to lend a book to a colleague when asked. Children observe the teacher saying something like: "I would love to lend you this book but we will be using it now," and then choosing a different book for circle time. Research shows that teachers call on boys to answer questions more often than they call on girls even when girls' hands are raised. Some of these teachers are aware of gender bias, and yet they behave in this manner (Wellhousen 1996, Greenberg-Lake 1994).

When I started teaching, I was uneasy interacting with girls. Delicate mannerisms and girlish behaviors made me uncomfortable. Later, when I went through analysis, I understood that my own discomfort related to dominant women in my childhood, difficulties I had with self-confidence, and even my sexuality. Exploring this area of my consciousness helped me become more accepting and at ease, and to feel closer to the girls in my class. All teachers experience favoring some children over others, even though many are reluctant to admit it. Teachers are taught that they must love all children equally. And yet, we all have biases and prefer some children to others. These biases may not only be related to cultural acceptance. For example, I knew a teacher who disliked one of the boys in her class. When she confronted this feeling in a support group setting she realized that the child reminded her of a man she once loved who had abandoned her. The realization deepened her self-understanding and she was able to interact with the boy in her class without confusing his behaviors with her past disappointments.

Unconsciously motivated behaviors affect our understanding of children even when we have acquired knowledge of child development. For example, wouldn't it be wonderful to celebrate with a two-year-old who defiantly says "no" to us? What a celebration of independence for her that could be! After all, a young child's defiance shows us that she is learning who she is, what her boundaries are, and what independence is about. She is testing her wings. It would be perfect to support and guide rather than punish her. We want girls to become determined and assertive, with a strong self-identity so that no one could ever put them down or limit their life opportunities anywhere again. Instead, many teachers and parents will label this defiant child and call her terrible two, stubborn, or willful. They might put her in time-out and scold her. They will probably do this even though they have learned that her behavior is typical and necessary for her development because she is a two-year-old.

Why do adults continue to behave in this manner, even though they have knowledge of child development? Most probably that's the way they were treated when they were children. There is no support for teachers to reflect specifically about how their childhood affects behaviors. They are not expected to hold still and think about where inappropriate reactions might come from. All the knowledge in the world about child development flies out the window as they instantly struggle to tame and clip the wings of our little freedom fighter. Many times when I talk to teachers about something like this, they are dismayed at themselves because they *know better*. And yet, their unconscious behavior continues. You see, self-reflection takes time and needs support. Such specific support is rarely given to teachers.

How I Came to Be Involved in This Work

> My hope is that each time you come upon a story of mine, you will turn inward and listen to a story told by your own inner voice . . . like the spider spinning her web, we create much of the outer world from within ourselves. (Steinem 1993, 8)

Who am I to be writing to you about confronting discomfort and becoming safe with bias and prejudice? After all, most people seem quite comfortable with their way of life and do not want to be told what to do regarding prejudice. In fact, most people seem to think they are not prejudiced at all. Perhaps if I share my story as an early childhood educator you might see some of yourself in me. I have learned so much from those who have shared their stories, and pain or suffering, with me over the years. As I tell you my history, I understand more deeply about myself. It becomes clearer where I developed my passion and concern about inequality and social injustice.

When we support each other through self-reflection, we are able to see ourselves in others and deepen an understanding of why we do what we do. By the way, children love to hear our stories, too. They learn about who we are, who they can be, and how to belong to the human species. They learn about feelings, perceptions, and experiences about adults.

I was born in Southern Rhodesia fifty-three years ago (as I write this manuscript). I was educated in the culture of a British colony. At school we would stand to sing the national anthem to the Queen of England and, in December, which was summer in Rhodesia, I would dream of white Christmases in my motherland of Great Britain even though my family was Jewish and atheist. When I was sixteen-years-old, the Rhodesian government unlawfully claimed its independence from Britain and began a regime of terror for liberal thinkers. Black Africans had no right to vote. They were employed mostly as servants for very little pay and had dire living conditions, on the very properties of the white African families for which they worked.

My own Nanny Margaret had to leave her children in a rural area far away in order to live on our property. Each day she would rise up at four or five in the morning so that she could bring us tea to our bedside to start the day. I always wondered about how she felt doing that, and I do not think I can even imagine how she must have missed waking up her own children to start their day with them. That memory haunts me even today as I write about it forty years later. It causes me pain to think about it. We seem to remember the small things, brief moments from childhood. Receiving tea each morning is nothing big or elaborate. However, there is depth and meaning to memories even though we might store them in our brains as something simple.

I still experience much guilt as I think of Margaret rising early to tend to my needs, forsaking those of her own children, for so little pay and having to live, literally, in my backyard in a primitive hovel without electricity. I do not know how I can ever make it up to her. I wish she could know that I wrote about it in this manuscript in America for early childhood teachers to read. Even though I was a child and had no role model to teach me different ways, I still experience shame about not having done it differently. Why didn't I rise early together with Margaret and share a cup of tea that sometimes she, and sometimes I, could have made? Or, why not allow her children to live with her? And what about renovating the run-down little shack in the backyard? As white Africans, we had choices. The adult white Africans could have taught their children differently.

For some reason, when I was a teenager, I had enough foresight to join up with youth organizations that influenced my becoming an activist against oppression. I spent many hours of after-school activities learning about human rights issues, the Holocaust, and ideals of a socialist kibbutz (commune-type agricultural settlement) movement in Israel, as well as participation in multiracial summer camps of people devoted to the freedom of Zimbabwe. I envisioned a world of freedom and equal opportunity for all. I was young and clumsy of my vision, though, and carried much learned prejudice with me on my journey into adulthood.

After awhile, because of what the government termed emergency laws, acquaintances were deported or house detained, and I no longer felt safe to stay in Rhodesia. Other friends and family were leaving the country for England or South Africa. Some of my friends and both my sisters went to Israel. In one of the organizations I belonged to, I had learned a love for Israel and, specifically, the life on kibbutz. I immigrated to Israel when I was nineteen where I became a preschool-kindergarten teacher with the Israeli Ministry of Education. My British upbringing was shocked into the reality of the in-your-face attitudes of a middle-eastern culture. Personal boundaries are defined differently from culture to culture, and in Israel, intrusion into one's personal space is the order of the day. In addition, people generally have a more direct approach in confronting each other about how they feel. For example, I had to unlearn how to stand in an orderly line to climb onto a bus. If I did not learn to push and shove I would never make it onto the bus in time for work. It became clear to me that each culture has a mode of behavior different from another.

Growing up in Zimbabwe, I had already begun to understand differences in culture from what I observed and from the behaviors of the significant adults in my life. Many black Africans I knew seemed to be more spontaneous and less subtle than the white Africans I grew up with. I still hear the sounds of Nanny Margaret singing as she worked. The continuous rhythm of her songs, as she scrubbed and cleaned, still ring in my ears and give me comfort to this day. In fact, whenever I hear Zulu songs I become choked up with tears of longing. I sang Zulu lullabies to my son for years as he grew up with me in Israel. I don't remember much kindness from the white Africans around me, including my family. They had wealth, servants, and all the leisure time in the world, and yet they seemed stern and punitive and not very accepting of others. So many even seemed dissatisfied with life. I remember kindness and expressions of joy as well as acceptance and forgiveness from Nanny Margaret and many other black African friends. And yet, they were extremely poor, were oppressed, and had so little leisure for themselves and their families.

Nan Partridge, author of *Not Alone: A Story for the Future of Rhodesia* (1972), is the mother of my best friend Jan. In my late teenage years they both influenced and reinforced for me that we all have choices to do things differently, to do what's right, and to make a stand against injustice. I realize now how fortunate I was to have been included in the lives of the Partridge family. They supported the gradual change in perception, of my worldview about social justice, freedom and, even, about religion.

> I am white; by colour, tradition and upbringing I belong to the small group [white Africans], which holds power. But I am deeply uneasy about this division, about this failure in understanding which continues, and will continue, because one group does not want to know the other. Tiny, determined, it holds onto its isolation stubbornly. And all the while its salvation lies in knowing. Even in the present, its peace lies in knowing many things, but not peace. "Uneasy lies the head" can be true of a group of people as well as of a king.
>
> The strength of the second group [black Africans] lies not so much in its numbers, because in some situations numbers can be meaningless, but in its great humanity. These are real people, sometimes great people, often good people; and their humanity, expressed partly in their joy in living, has proved stronger than the forces of destruction in the situation in which they find themselves. To recognize that humanity, that dignity, to salute it, to give it full expression, would change the face of this country, and its future. (Partridge 1972, 1–2)

As an early childhood teacher in Israel, I worked for the ministry of education for eleven years. My supervisor, Zehava, was born in Argentina. She had clear ideas about developmentally appropriate practices, aesthetic education, and acceptance of diversity. I learned about integrity and ethical conduct from her. She taught me that early childhood education is the most important profession in the world, that all cultures have an aesthetic beauty of their own, and that by participating in them we are all enriched. For example, when I celebrated Hanukkah with the children and families in my class, we learned about Hanukkah traditions of the Arab, African, and European Jewish people. She was a woman with strong principles and I learned from Zehava about standing up for what you believe in, and to never give in to mediocrity and boredom as a teacher. She taught me that children want and are able to learn about everything and anything.

Zehava would move us to classrooms in different areas of the city every couple of years. Each area was populated with a diverse group of Jewish people from different cultures, many of whom were from Arab countries like Syria, Egypt, Iraq, Yemen, Morocco, and Tunisia. Some were from Western-Anglo cultures. Teaching diverse populations, I learned never to assume anything about any one family and that each child I taught was completely unique. For some, I was completely unprejudiced because, in my childhood, I had not been taught to fear those cultures. It became clear to me that prejudice is learned and I began to notice comfort zones within myself regarding different cultures and behaviors. Being moved around in this manner, there was no time for boredom and I learned to be flexible and adjust to all kinds of situations.

As Israel is always in a state of war, each morning I would do a security check around the playground fence for dangerous mines camouflaged as fountain pens or other small objects. (I found a mine once and we all ran down to the bomb shelter while security police eliminated it.) Each country has its own safety regulations for young children. We did not conduct fire drills in Israel, however, bomb shelter drills were essential. I became accustomed to live with warlike conditions: very high taxes, bomb shelter drill sirens, and constant heightened awareness about packages left unattended. It took me almost two years of living in the United States to not jump up in alarm when I heard the fire engine sirens in our peaceful neighborhoods. To this day, I still look at unattended packages with caution. It is difficult to give up survival skills.

In 1988 I came to the United States. I was thirty-eight and divorced for a second time. My fifteen-year-old son, Gilad, accompanied me as I set out on a different journey: an academic one. I returned to college for a master's and a doctoral degree in early childhood education. I was anxious and excited. Once again I was setting out into the unknown. I would face different cultures, in terms of a new country and academia. I was taking a risk in uprooting Gilad and myself after living nineteen years in the Middle East. I think we have survived. It has been a struggle in so many ways and Gilad paid a high price for leaving behind peers and family during his sensitive teenage years.

I was faced, yet again, with culture shock in every way. This was a surprise to me as I had assumed that any English-speaking culture would be similar to my childhood British upbringing. Most of what I learned about the United States had been through books and television. I really did not know what to expect. At times it has been a struggle having people understand my British colonial accent. How different and interesting it has been! I am constantly fascinated about the dichotomous character of U.S. society. On the one hand, it is the land of freedom, democracy, and equal opportunity for all. On the other hand, there is a deep intolerance for diversity. In fact, we live in a society that is as ethnocentric and racist as it is democratic and free.

Many of the Asian students and parents I have encountered change their birth names and those of their children to American ones. They tell me it is in consideration of Americans, it is easier to pronounce. I understand how they feel in some ways. Hardly anyone spells or pronounces my name correctly. Somehow an extra *a* is added to the end of my name: Tamar—Tamar *a*. What's in a name? However, names are given at birth and for many of us our name has significance and is part of our identity. For example, 1949 was one year after the creation of the State of Israel when I was born in Southern Rhodesia. My father wanted to call me Dolores but my mother did not want my name to remind me of "sorrow." And so they chose a Hebrew name because they were excited about the promise of a newly formed Jewish State.

They chose excitement and promise for me rather than sorrow. I think of that sometimes. When people add an *a* to the end of *Tamar*, it becomes a Russian or an American name depending on the pronunciation. Learning the correct pronunciation of someone's birth name shows respect for people from different cultures.

Coming from the Middle East to the United States meant that I had to start learning different cultural behaviors. I have had many surprises along the way. One time I offered to share some mints with one of my professors. I had bought the mints to help ease a cough that was troubling me. He looked alarmed as I reached out the roll of mints: "Do I need that?" he asked with a frown. I was puzzled. "I don't know," I replied. "I thought you might like one." He explained to me that mints are used to ward off garlic or coffee breath. What a surprise for me! In the Middle East, garlic wards off the "evil eye." Our food is lavishly spiced with garlic and some people hang strings of garlic in their homes for good luck. I learned, then and there, that in the United States it is not good to smell of garlic, onions, or coffee and that I must be sure to remove spinach from between my teeth before I face the world outside my home.

During my second year in Buffalo, I supervised teachers in the university lab school. I remember one morning when a young woman came in with what seemed to me to be a smudge of dirt on her forehead. I leaned my body forward into her personal space and with a swift movement of my thumb tried to flick off the "dirt" saying, "What's this on your forehead?" She looked at me with a horrified expression on her face. "It is Ash Wednesday!" she replied. I then learned I cannot invade personal physical space by touching someone without permission and I learned about Ash Wednesday. Moving between cultures teaches us to respect different behaviors and customs.

On the one hand, the United States is the land of feminism and emancipation of women. On the other hand, I work in a profession made up of a majority of women who are underpaid and undervalued because they care for and educate young children. Patriarchy is the predominant societal system. It is not safe for women to walk alone in the streets at night. Women are battered in their own homes and still only receive seventy to eighty-five cents on each dollar that a man earns in the same positions (hooks 2000b). Feminism on one side, gender bias on the other—freedom and democracy on one side, segregation on the other, such contradictions!

According to Jonathan Kozol, we support and fund through tax dollars (or lack thereof) *Savage Inequalities*, thus segregating black and Hispanic from white children in public schools (1991). With the enormous disparity between urban and suburban public schools, some children are valued more than others. Some are worth $2,000 per year of public spending and others $11,000 (Kozol 1991). Is this unconscious societal bias or are we doing this to the children on purpose? How many of us are even aware that this is taking place? Kozol's book caused me much discomfort and pain. After I read it, I decided to stay in the United States for a while. There is much work to be done to overcome social injustice and segregation in our society.

> What startled me most—although it puzzles me that I was not prepared for this—was the remarkable degree of racial segregation that persisted almost everywhere . . . most of the urban schools I visited were 95 to 99 percent nonwhite. In no school that I saw anywhere in the United States were nonwhite children in large numbers truly intermingled with white children. (Kozol 1991, 2–3)

> Surely there is enough for everyone in this country. It is a tragedy that these good things are not more widely shared. All our children ought to be allowed a stake in the enormous richness of America. Whether they were born to poor white Appalachians or to wealthy Texans, to poor black people in the Bronx or to rich people in Manhasset or Winnetka, they are all quite wonderful and innocent when they are small. We soil them needlessly. (233)

The United States is a powerful nation dominating, affecting, and influencing the entire world. I think about how exciting it is for me to be here now amidst the power, struggle, discomfort, and pain. Perhaps my contribution to this society might be, in some way, to move us along toward understanding the freedom about the choices we make in our interactions with young children and families.

Talking about differences, eliminating stereotypes, and teaching activism to young children are some of the skills necessary for acceptance of diversity. Activism is an essential component in an anti-bias program. Taking a stand against discrimination strengthens self-identity and teaches children about integrity. There are different definitions and ideas about activism. Consciousness-raising and confronting the discomfort is a significant kind of activism, because each skill we struggle to acquire in educating acceptance causes discomfort at some level. People are not always well liked or popular for speaking out or taking a stand on controversial issues. If we have grown up practicing a color-blind approach, then talking about differences will feel uncomfortable. If we have learned to categorize people in order to understand who we are, eliminating stereotypes will feel unsafe. Taking action is risky business indeed.

What's Ahead?

The nature of bias is discussed in Chapter 2. Different scholars and theorists define bias and explore patriarchy and white privilege. There is a discussion about where bias comes from in a sociocultural context. The white patriarchal system, or dominant culture according to some theorists, has influenced our perceptions through our institutions in general and certainly the media. The major theme is there is one right way to be. Everything else is considered an *other* whether it relates to gender, ethnicity, or special needs. Bias is a large and diverse topic. It permeates all of our lives and perceptions and it is not only connected to culture or racism. There is bias about body weight or what we consider to be beautiful. Sexual orientation causes discomfort for many people. In the field of early childhood education, most of the teachers are women. We all experience and understand gender bias. Books upon books, and articles upon articles are written about how to include children with special needs into classrooms with typical children. This is a whole other subject of bias in and of itself.

Chapter 3 explores *how* we confront the personal discomfort that we feel from all the biases already mentioned. This chapter speaks to the core of the problem. Namely, we have learned biases from our families and society in order to survive. Now the challenge is to confront them and learn new and more effective survival skills that will help us negotiate our differences and truly practice acceptance. This is an idealistic chapter, however, there is hope and comfort in the end. Overcoming personal obstacles and strengthening human relationships are challenging and rewarding at the same time. We learn to develop compassion.

I have always been able to adjust quickly and learn the different cultural language of each situation wherein I find myself. When I use the term *culture* I am referring to family structures or where any group of people has joined together and created accepted norms for their behavior. Learning to belong to different family structures and cultures when I was very young through both of my parents' divorces and remarriages, I developed survival skills. I had to observe and listen carefully to what adults around me needed and how they felt. As I grew older, I took more risks and learned to ask a lot of questions of the adults in an attempt to understand why people do what they do. That way I felt safe, in control, and thought I was sure to get it right. In other words, I learned to do the things that would please them and in turn, hopefully, they would love me. Many young children learn similar survival skills.

Biases are learned at a very early age as survival skills. In order to be safe, our families and society have taught us to fear certain people and communities. We have been taught that our own culture is the right and safe path to take, while the cultures of others are not the road to salvation. As teachers of young children, we are expected to celebrate diversity. Acceptance of those who are other than us, different from us, requires us to give up those very survival skills we learned as young children, and replace them with those of the unknown—those, in fact, that we once were taught are dangerous. Giving them up is often difficult, and feels threatening and is sometimes impossible.

Many early childhood teachers seem to have low self-esteem. They do not value themselves, nor accept their own shortcomings. They feel like victims. Society has stamped the early childhood field with a judgment of something like "it's just women watching a bunch of kids." The judgment is concrete in terms of low pay and the fact that little higher education is required for childcare providers. Early childhood education is low in society's hierarchy of teaching as shown in a recent federal education bill where preschool is completely left out.

It is really difficult (sometimes impossible) to have a capacity to respect others if we do not respect ourselves or feel respected. Since anti-bias work has a lot to do with valuing and respecting the difference in others, what are we doing to address the issue of self-esteem for teachers of young children? After all, education and higher salaries take time to achieve. Confronting feelings of low self-esteem is uncomfortable and painful indeed. For many of us it is too uncomfortable to face. And so, we avoid, or worse still, deny it.

In Chapter 4, In and Out of Confidence, I explore the issue of self-esteem in-depth and at a personal level. It has been difficult for me to accept that I felt like a victim, in and out of confidence with myself. However, at a certain point in time, I realized that I have choices in my societal or worldview. I can choose not to feel like a victim. I have options in the way I value myself. Changing my perspective has given me the self-respect and confidence I need to accept others more comfortably. Education has played a major role for me about gaining confidence in myself as a professional in the early childhood field. We must require early childhood teachers to acquire higher education. Then, not only will they receive respectable salaries, but more important, gain the knowledge and understanding necessary to change perspectives about self and their worldview.

There is no safe place emotionally or physically in the education and development of teachers for confronting uncomfortable feelings they might have. When doing anti-bias work, issues arise that sometimes cause pain and anger. Counselors, for example, are able to refer clients to colleagues when they feel discomfort. In addition, they are able to seek counseling supervision when they need support with biases and appropriate interventions. It is not possible for teachers to refer children to their colleagues or seek counseling supervision in the context of education. Teachers just have to get on with it one way or another. As a result, young children are the recipients of many of our harmful, unconscious behaviors.

> The time has come to explode the "sham" of the neutral position, the clinical myth that it is possible for therapists not to introject their own values into therapy. Every therapist carries prejudices, beliefs, values, attitudes, and judgments into every session. These color everything that happens in a session from the kinds of questions that we ask to the hypotheses that we form and the interventions that we make. It is important that we hold our own values up to scrutiny. (Walters, Carter, Papp, and Silverstein 1988, 202)

Why would we think that teachers are different from the therapists in this statement? How can we expect early educators to be professional without providing them opportunities for holding their own values up to scrutiny, when they spend so much time with children modeling different behaviors that they are asked (sometimes required) to undertake (Meyer 1997)?

Self-reflection is a deceptive term because very often the most effective reflection happens when we share our ideas with others and develop dialogue. If teachers were given the opportunity to reflect with others about some of these uncomfortable feelings, they might be able to change their practices or biased behaviors in more authentic ways. Support is critical. Language and communication development (how to listen to others, how to tell *my* story) is an important component in anti-bias work as well. Listening to each other's stories helps us to understand how people develop survival skills so that we are better able to negotiate our differences. Through discussion we learn about ourselves.

In addition, as we work in and out of confidence with feelings of low self-esteem and some of us struggle to learn how to change our worldview, we could all do with support. Compassionate co-reflection can be supported with mentors, supervisors, colleagues, or support groups. In Chapter 5, I tell the story of an anti-bias support-supervision group that was created by early childhood teachers and administrators for the specific purpose of understanding personal bias. Portions of the chapter are drawn from my doctoral dissertation (Meyer 1997) and a paper presented at a recent symposium (Jacobson 2000).

We arrive at the final chapter: Courage and Compassion. Anti-bias work takes courage. It is a challenging and sometimes painful struggle to confront the discomfort that bias causes us. Acceptance of others requires us to respect differences and learn how to walk in another person's shoes. Developing empathy is necessary for compassion, which, according to Jersild, "is the ultimate expression of emotional maturity . . . is not the emotion of the weak . . . is the hard-gotten property of the strong" (Jersild 1955, 125–126).

> To be compassionate one must be able to accept the impact of any emotion—love or hate, joy, fear, or grief—tolerate it and harbor it long enough and with sufficient absorption to accept its

meaning and to enter into a fellowship of feeling with the one who is moved by the emotion. This is the heroic feature of compassion in its fullest development: to be able to face the ravage of rage, the shattering impact of terror, the tenderest promptings of love, and then to embrace these in a larger context, which involves an acceptance of these feelings and an appreciation of what they mean to the one who experiences them. (Jersild 1955, 125)

If you reach the final chapter and are ready to take on the challenge of confronting discomfort, you have courage and compassion indeed! We can start to clear the way for anti-bias and design together objectives of an ideal program. The concept of acceptance is foreign to most people. We are rewarded, punished, and judged from the day we are born. We have been taught to survive this way. The objectives of such a program would be to relearn some of these survival skills and really understand tolerance and acceptance. It is an ideal, of course.

However, we cannot afford not to be idealistic about it because, right now, people are treated unfairly on the basis of class, culture, sexual orientation, gender, abilities, and physical appearance. Often, the unfair treatment is unconscious to the perpetrator. The goal of this book is to create such an ideal program in our classrooms and schools. It is about having a vision that gives us the courage to face the discomfort within ourselves, and, thus, educate young children to develop a strong sense of self, have respect for others, and create a democratic and fair society with justice for all.

Reflections on Bias

2

As we prepare ourselves and the children we teach for the 21st century, can we, with our sisters and brothers in this, and every country around the world, build societies where diversity and equity thrive? Can we each learn how to live our own deeply felt beliefs and values while also respecting and supporting others to do the same? Can we figure out how to build social and economic institutions that do not rest on privilege for some at the expense and degradation of the many?"

Louise Derman-Sparks, "Educating for Equality: Forging a Shared Vision"

Examples of Bias

My husband and I have dinner with colleagues. We talk about how wonderful it is to walk in Delaware Park in Buffalo. Our colleague's wife becomes excited as she mentions meeting other people in the park. She says, "Every day, when I walk, I meet this interesting black couple and we always stop and talk."

I overhear women behind me as I take my daily walk. They are talking about a house that is for sale in their neighborhood. They mention that it costs $390,000 and one of the women says, "We are hoping that a nice family buys this one. It is next door to us."

I give a guest lecture to an undergraduate class about an anti-bias curriculum. I talk about *white privilege.* A young woman student suddenly says, "I hate Oprah!" "Really," I reply, "Why?" She says, "She's always pushing all that black issue stuff in our faces. I'm sick of hearing about it."

A male student, taking my child development class, asks me, "Dr. Jacobson, do you get mad when a man opens a door for you?" I laugh out loud. "No," I reply, "I did go through a period when I wanted to open the door for myself." "Why do women get mad at me for that? I'm just using common courtesy," he says.

The University at Buffalo Child Care Center (the program that I direct) considers collaborating with a local agency including children with special needs in our preschool program. One of our teachers says: "When will the *intrusion* program begin?" We laugh out loud as we realize her slip of the tongue. We wonder how it will be to include children identified with disabilities with our typical preschool children. We wonder how special education and our childcare teachers will work together as a team.

Each of the scenarios depict some form of bias. Why does our colleague's wife need to mention that the interesting couple is black? Is it unusual that a black couple is interesting? Does she want to impress me by saying that she is able to stand and talk to a black couple? Is she pleased with herself for overcoming discomfort in her relationships with people of color? Am I biased because of the way in which I hear her presumably innocent comment?

My bias about wealthy people in nice neighborhoods tunes my ear specifically to the conversation of those women in the park. I want to turn around and ask them, "What do you mean by nice? Do you mean wealthy, well-behaved, coming from a certain community, or the color of their skin? What do you *mean*?"

The young woman who hates Oprah does not want to hear about African American issues. She goes on to say that she was not responsible for slavery. My bias shone through in my interaction with her as I winced at her remarks. I wanted her to be accepting of others' pain and, in turn, I felt intolerant of her attitude. I want everyone to understand that racism is intolerable.

Gender bias is emotional for me. I came to feminism late in life and very often I need to think it out loud in order to strengthen my understanding of our society's patriarchal model. The student in my child development class senses this about me and asks his question. He is biased, too. He believes that a man should open doors for women. He cannot grasp why it should be a problem or an issue. He does not understand why women make such a fuss about a simple, common courtesy.

At our childcare center we laugh about how our colleague terms the inclusion program as *intrusion* at first. We are able to take that slip and turn it into a significant opportunity for an in-depth discussion about discomfort and fear surrounding inclusion and children with special needs. The more teachers are encouraged to explore their discomfort, the easier it becomes to let it go. When all types of teachers accept that all children have special needs then, perhaps, everyone would diversify and individualize teaching methods for all children. Thus, inclusion programs are more likely to succeed.

Every semester I teach a course in applied child development. A large part of the course is devoted to learning about an anti-bias curriculum. One of my assignments has the students visit card and toy stores in a popular mall and look at how diversity is handled. I have been giving students this assignment for about ten years, and the findings are always the same. In group dicussion, students express surprise and amazement at the level of awareness that they did not have before the exercise. They describe segregation in the toy and card stores, segregation of gender and culture. They find silence where cultures and different abilities are not represented at all.

Some of the things they say are: "We didn't expect that there wouldn't be cards or toys for specific types of people," "after going to the toy store, we realize how the store is segregated into boy and girl toys. Girls are supposed to bake, make jewelry, while boys are supposed to play with toys that involve using their hands (building with Legos, using action figures)," and "It makes me sad how and what we are telling our kids . . . what to buy, what is appropriate for girls and boys, and how they should look. . . . It is hard to buy cards for exactly what we want because there is little diversity. Cards go by the majority or what is popular but not what makes us different." Over and over again, during class discussions, we discover that popular consumer culture plays a large part in dictating segregation and prejudice about race, gender, and abilities.

The thesaurus has similes for *bias*: *prejudice, partiality, unfairness, favoritism, preconceived notion, foregone conclusion, predisposition, preconception, intolerance, bigotry, narrow mindedness, injustice,* and *discrimination*. In the *Anti-Bias Curriculum: Tools for Empowering Young Children,* bias is defined as: "Any attitude, belief, or feeling that results in, and helps to justify, unfair treatment of an individual because of his or her identity" (Derman-Sparks 1989, 3). As a result of these feelings, beliefs, and attitudes, individuals or groups of people are excluded, incarcerated, or even killed.

Bias is a part of every one of us and accompanies us throughout our lives. We are taught to discriminate from a very young age. While adults applaud preschoolers' ability to learn different colors, children are often silenced when they notice differences about people. We are taught bias in subtle and not so subtle ways. Often, it is through the silence of significant adults in our lives or their unease when talking to children about what they notice as different.

Growing Up in a Patriarchal System

I would like to make an assumption here as I write this. Teachers of young children do not want to treat children and families unfairly. They care about children and believe that prejudice is harmful, and want to see a better world, a changed world with freedom and equal opportunity for all. I would like to think that all early childhood professionals agree about this, at least in principle. However, it is difficult for teachers to be agents of change and confront a system that holds fast to the traditions of a patriarchal model. A model where relationships of competition, power, oppression, and domination control our society's economic, political, and cultural institutions. The patriarchal model affects everyone, men and women alike.

From the day we are born, we are taught and socialized by our families, media, popular culture, and schools to participate in this system. In Western culture "educated white men's views guide the beliefs and structures that cement the dominant culture. Thus, for example, the world of work is considered more noble and more real than the world of home and hearth because paid work has been men's sphere" (Debold, Wilson, and Malave 1993, 6–7).

bell hooks describes the "strongest patriarchal voice" in her life as that of her own mother (hooks 2000b). In *Mother Daughter Revolution: From Betrayal to Power*, mothers are described as the gatekeepers of patriarchy once young girls reach adolescence (Debold, Wilson, and Malave 1993). " 'Good mothering' as it now exists for mothers and daughters guarantees that a daughter is abandoned by the women closest to her at the door to patriarchy" (29). As culture has prescribed it, mothers teach daughters to fit in. Everyone is taught to participate in a patriarchal model.

Michael Moore describes women's participation in patriarchy. He notes,

> Then in 1920, just to show women we're good sports, we gave them the right to vote. And guess what? *We remained in power!* . . . Suddenly, women had more votes; they could have thrown our collective male ass into the political trash heap. But what did they do? They voted for *us!* How cool is that? Have you ever heard of any group of oppressed people that suddenly, by their sheer numbers, takes charge—and then votes in overwhelming numbers to keep their oppressors in power? (2001, 149)

Even more interesting (or alarming) are Moore's list of statistics. After more than eighty years with the right to vote, and

> despite the growth of the massive women's movement—here's where we stand . . . not a single woman has been on the ballot of the major parties for President or Vice President in twenty of the twenty-one national elections since 1920 . . . there are only five women governors in fifty states; women hold only 13 percent of the seats in Congress, 496 of the top 500 companies in America are run by men; just four of the top twenty-one universities in the United States are run by women . . . women's earnings average 76 cents for every $1 earned by men. (Moore 2001, 149–150)

Even though women might have come a long way in the last thirty years their lives seem to have become more difficult and complicated (Greer 1999). In fact, according to Germaine Greer, "It's time to get angry again." There seem to be many contradictions facing women in today's society:

> The career woman does not know if she is to do her job like a man or like herself? Is she supposed to change the organization or knuckle under to it? Is she supposed to endure harassment or kick ass and take names? Is motherhood a privilege or a punishment? . . . On every side speechless women endure end-

less hardship, grief and pain, in a world system that creates billions of losers for every handful of winners. (Greer 1999, 3)

Participation in a patriarchal model is very subtle. It can be the choice of books we read to young children. For example, have you ever read *The Giving Tree* by Shel Silverstein? For some, I have heard that it is their very favorite book, read to them since early childhood. Look at it closely as it begins: "Once there was a tree and she loved a little boy." From the outset, it establishes gender roles, and so it continues. The tree awaits the boy for days, weeks, and years. She awaits him as he becomes a man, or returns from a journey, challenging and interesting, far away. Her role is to wait for him, please and give him her all until she is stripped to nothing—a mere stump—for him to sit upon as an old man. Over and over again throughout the book, her waiting is filled with expectation of his return, "and then one day the boy came back and the tree shook with joy." She suffers with loneliness as she waits, but it seems worth it when he finally shows up. The boy, on the other hand, climbs, adventures, builds, travels, comes and goes, takes and takes and takes. Each time the boy strips away another layer of her, Shel Silverstein tells us, "And the tree was happy."

The model becomes clear. Was Shel Silverstein aware of gender roles when he wrote this book in the early sixties? Who knows?

> Where I come from, Shel Silverstein was a demigod. I come from Chicago. We high school kids would see him on State Parkway and say, "Do you know who that is. . . ." And we all knew who it was. He was Hugh Hefner's sidekick, he was the great cartoonist, he lived with Hef at the Playboy Mansion, in a riot of delight. (Mamet 2001)

Silverstein began as a writer and cartoonist for *Playboy* magazine in the 1950s. Perhaps, when he wrote *The Giving Tree* in 1963, he was thinking about himself and his mother, or himself and his favorite tree, or the beauty of love and sacrifice, just as so many children's books develop, unconsciously reinforcing gender-biased roles of our society. After all, the story is left to our own interpretation.

After reading the book to students one evening, I reflected on how I had asked the students to listen with gender roles in mind. When I completed the book and looked up, I saw many of the women's faces staring at me with anger and indignation. Some had tears in their eyes. I wondered about their indignation and angry comments as I thought about the story of *The Giving Tree*, who lives only to please the boy. She does everything to make him happy. She gives away everything she has for his satisfaction: branches, leaves, apples, and even her entire trunk. Time after time, the tree is described as trembling with joy when the boy finally shows up after long periods of being gone. Isn't that exactly what we have been socialized to believe? The woman's role is to do everything in her power to please her "boy" and sacrifice everything to make him happy. Women should feel excited, even grateful, when a man expresses interest in her. Furthermore, his interest should make her feel special, needed, and worthwhile. It took decades of re-education and reflection for me to realize that I have a different option. I can choose not to feel that way. Naomi Wolf writes about some of the confusing messages she received growing into a young woman:

> We needed space so badly. When we discovered that, if we went with boys, space would open up for us, we found to our surprise, that we needed boys. And yet boys were part of the danger. Thus, our balance of power with boys was thrown off. This inequity regarding moving fast into the world was the first real lesson I had about the inequities between men and women. We needed boys more than they needed us. We were more scared of them physically than they were of us. We did not know this, but we probably even desired them as much or even more than they desired us. If we chose not to go with them, we couldn't go at all. But they were always free to choose to go without us. (Wolf 1997, 34)

Surely, there are other ways that women and men can achieve equality of relationships. Women and men have other options. Or do they? For we keep on reading *The Giving Tree* types of books to our little girls and boys, without thinking about how we are reinforcing these roles as if that's the way it has to be.

In the child development class we do an exercise with children's literature where each student brings in three or five books they loved when they were young. We count up the total number of children's books in a class of forty-five undergraduate students. Then, we look at how many of them have stories with male or female heroes and what their roles typically are. About 90 percent of the books have male heroes and the roles are usually stereotypical. That means the male heroes are adventurous, courageous, solve problems, and are allowed or expected to be naughty or mischievous. The female roles are nurturing. They typically take care of others, cook, clean, or behave in gentle and cute ways. Whether the characters in the children's books are children themselves or little furry animals like rabbits, kittens, or puppies, the gender roles are always clear.

Women and men participate in a patriarchal model through literature and the media in our society. We do not have to give up reading classics, like *The Giving Tree*, or shopping in popular stores. However, we are able to become more aware that perceptions and biases are learned through direct and subtle messages within our culture and society. Sharing a different point of view or allowing discussions with diverse opinions challenges us to develop different perceptions. For example, we might read a book like *The Giving Tree* and then give an option for discussion of "what if the tree, in the story, was male (he) and the boy was a girl (she)?" We need not be victims of patriarchy. We can unlearn it. We have a choice.

Many years ago I read a book that described men and women creating a new societal model together and changing from dominance and power to relationships of *interdependence* or "equality" (Clinebell 1973).

> Certainly it means that both sexes will have to give up some things. Men will have to give up dependence on women as an automatic servant class and will have to move over to make room for women in public life. Women will have to give up their helplessness and dependence for identity on men . . . it means hanging loose about sex roles, what Maslow describes as a "desexualizing of the statuses of strength and weakness, and of leadership so that either man or woman can be, without anxiety and degradation, either weak or strong, as the situation demands. Either must be capable of both leadership and surrender." (Clinebell 1973, 31–32)

The title of the book, *Meet Me in the Middle* aptly describes the notion that men and women can be equal though different. As Bruce

Perry would say: "we've invented the way we live, we can change the way we live" (Perry 2002).

Anti-bias and Antiracist Education

Over the last sixty years, not only have researchers established the fact that young children have accurate knowledge about the evaluations that society makes of different racial and ethnic groups, but they have also established that by the age of four most white children have developed strong in-group preferences and negative attitudes toward other racial groups (Banks 1993). By implementing well-developed curriculum interventions, educators can help young children develop more positive racial behaviors and attitudes. According to Banks, teacher-educators will have to assist teachers in acquiring skills, knowledge, and attitudes if they are to function effectively in a multicultural classroom. Teachers are the "key variable" in implementing diversity education and they are "human beings who bring their cultural perspectives, values, hopes, and dreams to the classroom. The teacher's values and behaviors strongly influence the views, conceptions and behaviors of young children" (Banks 1993, 248).

Anti-bias is another way of describing a multicultural curriculum. Both attempt to teach children about accepting differences in others. Most multicultural curriculum materials tend to stress only ethnic culture whereas an anti-bias curriculum addresses different kinds of bias including gender, sexual orientation, culture and abilities addressing all the *-isms*. There are many guides and materials relating to multicultural curriculum today. From the way in which they are constructed, they can be categorized into two paradigms: *Tolerance* or *Transformation* (Derman-Sparks 1998, 2). Derman-Sparks holds fast to the "transformation paradigm," calls on all teachers who practice multicultural education "to place their work in the larger context of societal change," and invites them to "work both within and outside their classrooms as advocates and activists for the conditions in which all children can grow to their fullest, wonderful potential" (3).

Sonia Nieto differentiates between the concepts of tolerance and acceptance (Nieto 1998). "When we think of what tolerance means in practice, we have images of a grudging but somewhat distasteful acceptance. To tolerate differences means that they are endured, not necessarily embraced" (10). *Acceptance*, on the other hand seems to be a different stage in supporting diversity and "implies that differences are acknowledged and their importance is neither denied or belittled" (11). This, to Nieto, is a "substantial movement toward multicultural education" (11). It is not enough to celebrate different holidays, hang up posters, or display dolls representing diverse cultures. Both Nieto and Derman-Sparks, through "acceptance" or "the transformation paradigm," call on educators of multicultural or antibias curriculum to become activists and advocates of change.

Many white teachers have had little, if any, training or development in antiracist education (Lawrence and Tatum 1998). From the limited available studies, it seems some white teachers develop positive feelings toward people of color after participation in multicultural programs while few have been influenced in making a significant change in teaching practices (1998, 45). Lawrence and Tatum discuss the development of white racial identity as an integral part of anti-racist education, "for whites, the process involves becoming aware of one's 'whiteness,' accepting this aspect of one's identity as socially meaningful and personally salient, and ultimately internalizing a realistically positive view of whiteness which is not based on assumed superiority" (45).

In "White Privilege: Unpacking the Invisible Knapsack" (1988), Peggy McIntosh describes learning about racism as reinforcing her thinking of others as disadvantaged. It was surprising for her when she realized that, in fact, it put her at an advantage. She writes about being "newly accountable" when discussing white privilege:

> My schooling gave me no training in seeing myself as an oppressor, as an unfairly advantaged person, or as a participant in a damaged culture. I was taught to see myself as an individual whose moral state depended on her individual moral will . . . whites are taught to think of their lives as morally neutral, normative and average, and also ideal, so that when we work to benefit others, this is seen as work which will allow "them" to be more like "us." (1)

Assumed superiority for whites is very much a part of one's identity in a society of white privilege. How could it not be? My high school friend, Jan, wrote to me after attending the Nongovernmental

Organization Forum conference parallel to the United Nation World Conference against Racism in Durban, South Africa:

> We white westerners are not racists because we wish ill toward people different from us but because we have benefited from a racist system which has advantaged us on the plunder and prof-its made by the West over the last centuries, that we continue to make and regard as rightfully ours. Growing up in Zimbabwe, I as a white child had sums spent on my education 14 times greater than the sum spent on a black child. That is one way to quantify my debt, and now I can work out how to use my wealth, education and privilege to promote basic human rights for every-one, especially the right to self-determination. Every act of soli-darity with the oppressed is a step forward. (Delacourt e-mail to author 2001)

Jan's words support my constant thoughts about the guilt and shame of growing up and participating in an unjust society and ben-efiting so much on the backs of others. These are feelings, it seems, that I will always carry with me and must never forget. The guilt and shame is part of the discomfort I have to face even though it is pain-ful. However, it deepens an understanding of myself and, thus, I be-come freer to make different choices.

Just as women struggle to find their own voice within the frame-work of a patriarchal societal model, so do people of color with re-gard to white privilege. Recently, I participated in an antiwar rally and heard a young African American student recite a poem he had just written about democracy. The poem moved me by the way it expresses how racism causes people anger and pain:

America

A land for the free?
Why no free for me?
Is my color a crime, what did it do?
Did my soul sin before I was born?
Why does democracy seem likes it's mocking me?
Is it just that "Every man created equally" includes
everybody except those of us considered nobody?
Don't look away!
Don't put your head down!

Don't turn away from me!
Look me in the eye and tell me to my face:
Why am I brutalized and utilized?
Do you hold something to gain?
Is it because of the $\frac{3}{5}$'s of human in me,
that I get a fraction of your freedom?

Marquis Woolford 2002

Michael Moore traces white privilege in the United States to the legacy of slavery:

> African Americans *never* got the same fair start the rest of us got. Their families were willfully destroyed. Their language and culture and religion were stripped from them. Their poverty was institutionalized. . . . The America we've come to know would never have come to pass if not for the millions of slaves who built it and created its booming economy. (Moore 2001, 69)

One of the students in my class described a person who does not fit a white, patriarchal model as being considered deviant. She was referring to anyone from an ethnic culture that is considered minority such as African American, Latino, Native American, or Asian. No one wins from a societal model that excludes others or considers them deviant because of gender, color, sexual orientation, different abilities, weight, religion, culture, or anything else for that matter. Bias is pervasive. It is the incorrect presumption that everyone should be like me, everyone should think like me. The president of the Children's Defense Fund, Marian Wright Edelman, writes:

> It is utterly exhausting being black in America—physically, mentally, and emotionally. While many minority groups and women feel similar stress, there is no respite or escape from your badge of color. . . . It can be exhausting to be a black student on a "white" college campus or a black employee at a "white" institution where some assume you are not as smart as comparable whites. The constant burden to "prove" that you are as smart, as honest, as interesting, as wide-gauging and motivated as any other individual tires you out—as does the need to decide repeatedly whether you'll prove to anybody what they have no right to assume or demand. (Edelman 1993, 23–24)

Accepting Diversity

In the early education profession there is much talk about celebrating diversity. It is difficult for people to authentically celebrate that which they do not accept or, more important, fear. More than anything, we have to learn to simply face the fact that everyone is different in some way. Within every group of people there are differences. It is a fact of life. Nieto reminds us that grudgingly enduring differences is what some of us have been doing for a long time. Acceptance is quite a different matter.

Within less than forty years, over fifteen states will find between 50 and 70 percent of their population to be non-Anglo (Garcia and McLaughlin 1995). Over the past thirty years Americans still do not accept the cultural and linguistic diversity among them and continue to perceive minority populations as "lazy, less intelligent and of lower moral character" (ix). This is frustrating in view of the fact that this is after millions of dollars and hours of dedicated work in addressing injustice and inequalities through decades of civil rights, a women's movement, and an equal educational opportunity initiative (ix).

Stereotyping, for example, causes teachers to overlook Asian American children in the belief that they all will do well at school, reward African American girls for nurturing behavior only, or think that Native American children are all nonverbal (Delpit 1995). Delpit expresses concern about how poor people and people of color might define themselves when that definition "involves a power that lies outside of the self. It is others who determine how they should act, how they should be judged. When one 'we' gets to determine standards for all 'wes,' then some 'wes' are in trouble!" (xv). Jonathan Kozol calls on policy makers to examine the way education is funded for children of different ethnic groups and economic classes (Kozol 1991). Most public schools in the United States remain more segregated and unequal than in 1954, according to Kozol. Some educators believe that terms used by teachers and schools are unconsciously racist:

> terms such as "at risk" and "culture of poverty" hide the insidious racism that underlies much of our social relations. As Sonia Nieto has stated, "Students' ethnicity . . . is consciously or un-

consciously used by schools and teachers as an explanation for either their success or lack of success at school." (Kenyatta and Tai 1997, viii)

In 1998, a small group of national leaders sponsored and supported by the National Association for the Education of Young Children (NAEYC) and W. K. Kellogg Foundation came together and created the document *Children of 2010* (Washington and Andrews 1998). They describe their dialogue, research, and debate about a number of issues including democracy, diversity, and demographics, as well as suggestions for best practices including "movements to change society." The authors write a letter to the children of 2010 in which they share their reflections and vision as a conclusion to the report.

According to Washington and Andrews, the Hispanic population will "rise dramatically, particularly in the southwest and west, where Latinos will constitute a majority of the population in some states. The African American population will increase representing a majority . . . in certain southern states. Asian Americans will also constitute a larger share of the overall U.S. population" (1998, 157). Population growth is further explained by an influx of immigration from Asia and Latin America as well as higher fertility rates for people of color "compared to non-Hispanic Whites." The Letter to the Children of 2010 addresses the issue of respect:

> Our notion of *respect* is more than simply being polite. It acknowledges and values individuality. Respect searches for appropriate, individualized responses to each person's uniqueness. . . . We hope to make both ourselves and our institutions more respectful of and responsive to individual differences. This must address the problem of unequal access to opportunity, for each one of you has a right to reach for the American dream. Further, we believe that creating *fair access to opportunity* will benefit every child in America. There are so many physical differences, learning styles, interests and abilities among all children! Each of you deserves the respect of an individualized response that gives you access to your wonderful potential. (Washington and Andrews 1998, 158)

Endorsing Anti-Bias or Multicultural Education

The National Association for the Education of Young Children (NAEYC) actively endorses an anti-bias curriculum that supports children in developing their own individual and cultural identity while learning to respect other people whose experiences or values might be different from their own. The organization developed criteria for accreditation in the early 1980s (Bredekamp and Glowacki 1996). Based on an understanding that quality of care and education is associated with better outcomes for children and the need to improve early childhood programs, NAEYC has two major goals for the accreditation project: "to help program personnel become involved in a process that will facilitate real and lasting improvements in the quality of the program, and evaluate the quality of the program for the purpose of accrediting those programs that demonstrate substantial compliance with criteria for high quality" (Bredekamp and Glowacki 1996, 2). Three of the criteria for validation of accreditation encompass culturally appropriate, anti-bias educational practice. These are: staff treats children of all races, religions, family backgrounds, and cultures equally with respect and consideration; provides children of both sexes with equal opportunities to take part in all activities; and respects cultural diversity (*Accreditation Criteria and Procedures of the National Academy of Early Childhood Programs* 1998).

Goals are outlined for early childhood programs that foster each child's construction of a knowledgeable, confident self-identity; children's comfortable empathic interaction with diversity among people; children's critical thinking about bias; and each child's ability to stand up for herself and others in the face of bias (NAEYC 1995). They note that "culture in the classroom is not a topic that you have the privilege of adding or deleting. Culture is always present whenever humans interrelate with one another" (6).

From Awareness to Action

In some programs, early childhood educators are required to embrace a multicultural, anti-racist curriculum in their classrooms. Some teacher-educators and supervisors expect their students and teaching staff to do more than use appropriate multicultural materials in the classroom. They believe that teachers must become activists and make a stand for social justice. Indeed, there is no doubt that social change is imperative in order for all people to be treated fairly and equitably. Stories people tell about their life experience reinforce the literature and facts that many are discriminated against and excluded from fair access to opportunity. We are all products of a white patriarchal system. Early education and a powerful acculturation process have socialized us to accept and participate in this "damaged culture" (McIntosh 1988).

Awareness and information about bias and prejudice are important in helping teachers understand the need for change. There are organizations, books, and teacher education programs that instruct teachers about diversity and cultural acceptance giving them some support in multicultural education. Activism and taking a stand demands more from teachers than they are often able to take on. Discomfort is a significant obstacle and stands in the way of many well-intentioned persons, no matter who they are or the color of their skin.

I have been working for social justice since I was sixteen years old. My activism has included joining and serving organizations, reading, studying, educating, writing, attending rallies, and donating monies. However, self-reflection has been (and still is) the best resource for understanding myself in relation to bias and clearing the way for anti-bias work. It is not something I do now and again. It is a crucial component in supporting my work, and causes me discomfort more often than not. Once I started to confront my own prejudices, there was no turning back. Reflection affects and improves my interactions with teachers, children, and families. At times it is exciting and challenging, and at others it includes guilt and even embarrassment at myself. These feelings have often blocked me in making changes in my relationships.

Uncomfortable Feelings

I used to introduce myself as having been born in Zimbabwe. In fact, I was born in Southern Rhodesia, which became Zimbabwe much later in my life. Recently, when this was brought to my attention, I felt uncomfortable indeed. After some reflection, I realized that I had been denying the country where I was born. Had I been lying to people about where I was born? I contacted an old high school friend, Jan, and asked her why she, too, refers to herself as having been born in Zimbabwe when in fact she was born in Southern Rhodesia. She replied, "For me too it is unthinkable to say I grew up in Rhodesia! I suppose the dream was always for liberation."

I had been lying to myself for years. I had chosen to identify with a dream instead of reality by hiding behind pieces of my life because of feelings of guilt and shame that were hard to face. Accepting pieces of my childhood has been difficult. I was eager for Rhodesia to achieve independence and felt shame about participating in an unjust society. I had to take ownership of the fact that I was privileged just because of the color of my skin. This is painful even though as a child I was helpless at affecting any systemic change. These feelings accompany me as I travel through different lands and when I am with different groups of people. A large piece of who I am has to do with how I grew up. The feelings cloud my vision and influence my beliefs, values, and interactions, and at times they create an obstacle in my anti-bias work. Ultimately, however, they help me see more clearly.

As we search within ourselves for answers, we are faced with apprehension about how we solved problems or made decisions based on our childhood influences. Sometimes we feel anger about how helpless we were as children if we experienced injustice or discrimination. Each of us deals with discomfort in different ways. In the following chapter, I explore this aspect of anti-bias/antiracist work. We will discover how we learned those survival skills from our families and communities when we were young children. We will not only be able to imagine a world like the one that follows that bell hooks suggests to us, but we can take action in ways that will create social change for future generations.

> Imagine living in a world where there is no domination, where females and males are not alike or even always equal, but where a vision of mutuality is the ethos shaping our interaction. Imagine living in a world where we can all be who we are, a world of peace and possibility. Feminist revolution alone will not create

such a world; we need to end racism, class elitism, imperialism. But it will make it possible for us to be fully actualized females and males able to create beloved community, to live together, realizing our dreams of freedom and justice, living the truth that we are all "created equal." (bell hooks 2000b, x)

Confronting Our Discomfort

3

Clearing the Way

Even with support and validation, change is a voyage into the unknown. Even when our minds and hearts say that change is for the better, change requires that we let go of who we are and of our deepest assumptions about life. In between living as we were and realizing the new, we hang suspended in midair like trapeze artists waiting to be caught.

Elizabeth Debold, Marie Wilson, and Idelisse Malave, *Mother Daughter Revolution*

If you allow yourself to experience these sensations of discomfort—both physically and emotionally, while identifying their emotional origins—you will gradually begin to fear them less and less. Dealing with these feelings and allowing them to help you create changes in your life is your path to ultimate freedom.

Bob Greene, *Get with the Program!*

Exploring the Discomfort

Time and again I hear early childhood teachers say that they chose this profession because they love children. I question them about that. "Do you love *all* children?" I ask. "How can you love *all* children?" Some insist they love all children equally. Most of them bow their heads and snicker a little, embarrassed, as if caught with a secret. I was a teacher of young children for many years. I know that my interactions have not always been the most loving. I often observe teachers interacting with children in ways that do not seem loving to me.

A child runs enthusiastically to the sandbox in her classroom and reaches out gleefully to feel the sand sift through her fingers. A teacher barks, "Don't get the sand on the floor!" The child withdraws into her-self. I observe her suck in her breath and surround her chest slightly with her arms. After a few minutes, she walks away from the sand-box to find something else to do, something that will not get her into trouble before she has even begun. A toddler with Down syndrome cries uncontrollably when her special education teacher pulls her away from her primary caregiver in the midst of their playing together. The teacher is taking the child to work on different skills she needs to acquire. As the child cries, the teacher says firmly, "There's nothing to cry about. Nothing's wrong." The child continues to cry and is told this repeatedly. A child runs up to show the teacher a drawing she has been working on for over half an hour. The teacher exclaims, "How cute! My what a pretty dress you have on today!" It makes me feel uneasy when I observe children not having their feelings validated or acknowledged, or worse, seeing them humiliated.

The pain I feel when I observe these interactions is sometimes so intense that I retire to my office, close the door, and weep. And as I weep I reflect about myself when I was a little girl. I want to cry out, "Relate to that person! Validate her feelings! Take her seriously! Find out more about her ideas and what she might be thinking. Be kind!" I realize that when I was a child I could never have said those things to my mother or teachers even though I must have felt them over and over again. The discomfort is more than caring about children I ob-serve. It is about me.

I take my childhood with me into every area of my teaching. Time and again, I find myself trying to compensate for my feelings of guilt and shame whenever I am in the presence of brown-skinned people, whether they are from Africa, the Americas, or Europe. It is a constant struggle. At the same time, there is a part of me that really does not want to lose that privilege. The dilemma is how to share the privilege fairly with everyone. Sometimes I am aware of my discomfort and often times I am not. When I am aware, I am able to empathize with people different from me. However, when I behave unconsciously, I have no idea how other people feel. The discomfort causes anxiety and then I am unable to focus on anyone other than myself. I become blinded by my own feelings of discomfort.

At a workshop I gave recently, one of the attendees asked if I thought there was a difference between acknowledging the differences in others and accepting them. When I said I thought there was, she qualified the difference for herself by asking, "If I can accept the difference can I even be comfortable to disagree with people who are other than me?" I agreed enthusiastically. "Yes!" I replied, expanding on her question by describing some of my thoughts, "I can feel relaxed in those people's company, not need them to like me, nor think that I am okay, unbiased and a good, fair person in every way!"

Early childhood experiences set the stage for a person's social, emotional interactions and relationships as an adult. I was born between my mother's first and third marriages, which, in my family, have always been considered the important ones. My mother's marriage to my father was short, painful, and filled with conflict. When I was four years old my parents divorced. All of my siblings are half brothers and sisters. Four of them were from my mother's marriages. Three were from my father's first marriage, prior to marrying my mother. I have always felt that my mother's first and third husbands were the most meaningful to her, and I was a progeny of a relationship that seemed like a big mistake. Through the years, stories I heard about my father and his family were rarely respectful or positive. I learned to love and long for him in secret. He was fifty-five when I was born and, to me, felt like a kindly grandfather. I experienced him as a gentle man, a connoisseur of good food, who spoke many different languages, and delighted in my company.

My three older siblings have always been a tight-knit group for me. Their father (the first husband) is respected in my family as intellectual and financially successful. On the other hand, my father was considered miserly, moody, and culturally different from my mother's family. All three of my mother's husbands were Jewish. Two were Ashkenazi Jews of East European origin. My father was Sephardic, born in Rhodes Island, Greece. As Sephardic Jews originated in North Africa, they were often considered culturally inferior to many members of the Ashkenazi group. Some have even been called "black Jews" in a derogatory way.

My younger brother is from my mother's third marriage, which was once described by a member of the family as being like "the king, queen and crown prince." Since I was very young my mother seemed to devote most of her emotional energy to her third husband. Theirs was a passionate relationship that lasted almost forty years. My mother doted on my youngest brother, her fifth child. To this day he still lives on her property with his wife and three children.

Within my family I spent my life trying to find a place where I could feel respected and that I belonged. Mostly I felt like an ugly duckling whose egg had landed in the nest by accident. I was identified with the Sephardic culture, which my mother considered as a flaw in my personality. She stated to me a number of times that there was a black star over my head, which seemed to be leading me to ultimate disaster. Apart from trying to overcome deep feelings of alienation and worthlessness, I spent much of my childhood observing and listening, trying to fit into the different familial groups of siblings and fathers. I realized later that those situations were useful to me. In fact, I had been honing skills for cultural awareness and acceptance.

Growing up in my family of origin influenced my feelings and perceptions about bias. I felt unimportant, marginalized, and unworthy. As a result, I developed empathy for people who feel excluded. Longing to belong is at the core of my life script, and is painful for me. Therefore, I often find myself struggling to fit in with different groups, families, and cultures so that I might gain a sense of belonging, sometimes without purpose. These experiences, though, have made it easy to adjust to a variety of cultures and make acceptance of differences less uncomfortable for me than many other people I know. I have become more confident to make different choices that are healthier for me. Mostly, I have chosen to adjust to differences by developing empathy and flexible social skills.

Human beings have complex and diverse ways of dealing with emotional experiences learned in early childhood. For many years I chose to feel angry, vengeful, and bitter toward my family because of the painful emotions I experienced growing up. I am not sure when I made the decision to view my life with all its complex and diverse feelings as exciting and challenging. It took much reflection and soul searching. It is still painful at times when I feel unsure about where to fit in and how I belong within my family or other cultures. It takes courage to confront my discomfort. I have to face it over and over again.

When I was invited to hike across the Yorkshire Moors with my three older siblings I was ecstatic. I felt a glimpse of the fulfillment of the dream, finally, of being accepted and as belonging. As I look back and try to understand how my mother navigated her difficult life, I realize that overall she had a will to maintain family bonds between her children and her. My mother is a courageous woman who was self-taught and, in her way, has always advocated for children's rights. She was a white, privileged homemaker in Rhodesia. Yet she managed to share with us a politically liberal point of view. This dichotomy was typical in many white, privileged, "liberal" homes in Rhodesia. I believe that I inherited her strength of will and love of life. It has helped me come to terms with my painful childhood and admire her, as my therapist "Bob" would say, as "a work of art," pieces of which have become part of me.

Developing Survival Skills

Young children learn to survive by expanding their comfort zone. Becoming curious, they set out to discover new things. New discoveries are exciting and pleasurable but at the same time they are fraught with unease and fear. Children become familiar with the new discovery and then set out once again to challenge their comfort zone. Most of what we learned was acquired unconsciously, through trial and error, by observing significant adults in our lives navigating fears of discomfort and stress. We learned to survive in our family systems and communities. Our survival depended on doing the right things so that people we cared about would like us. Adults around us taught us what was safe or dangerous through their praise, admonishments, and silence. Nonverbal communication is subtle. It could be a tightening of the lips, an angry or anxious glance, slight shifting of the body, or a foot quivering back and forth. Children quickly learn to differentiate between the nonverbal cues that are safe or not reliable. They make assumptions based on what they sense unless we are explicit in what we mean.

Our survival depended upon learning about the cultural mores of our family and community: how to sit and eat at the table, what to say when, how to say it, when to be silent, how to behave with strangers or different family members, what attitudes to have about school, who we could like and dislike, and so on. When we meet people from cultures with different worldviews from us, we immediately feel unsafe. It is as if we have to give up what we learned to survive in order to open ourselves to different cultural mores. We are not sure of how other people will behave or interpret what we say. A lot of the time we do not understand them at all. That makes us uneasy and anxious. This discomfort blocks us from making the changes necessary to allow fair opportunity for everyone. In order to feel safe we fall back on stereotyping, categorizing, and labeling groups of people. We prejudge motives, beliefs, and behaviors and create a large block of people to fear or think are weird and strange. There is no chance for individuality in our mind's eye. It becomes us versus them.

Adults taught us bias for survival when we were very young. From the day we were born, significant adults in our lives have tried to keep us safe. In the first three years of life we set down memory for the rest of our lives. Emotional memory is developed in the brain from the beginning of life. In fact, the brain develops up to 85 percent of its final structure within the first three years of life (Perry 2001). Perry reminds us that our biases are not genetic. They are something we learn during our earliest years. We are taught to be alert to what is safe and dangerous. Throughout our childhood, adults share with us their fears, aspirations, values, beliefs, and ways of solving problems. According to Alice Miller, "messages the brain receives in those formative years may imprint themselves more indelibly than any other information it will ever be required to process" (Miller 2001, 114).

Life experience taught our caregivers what worked and what to be wary of in order to succeed. Some life experiences might have included traumatic events that we never had to face. For example, Holocaust survivors experienced being rounded-up, pushed into trains, having numbers burned into their arms, and waiting to be executed in gas chambers. Most of us never experienced any intensity of fear like that. People who survived the Great Depression will have a perspective about life that is different from those who have never known hunger, desperation, and deprivation. People who have experienced great loss or humiliation pass on their fears and survival skills to children even though those skills might not be necessary any longer for a younger generation. While these examples might seem extreme, the main point is that, at a subtle level, whatever we experienced as children, we are probably going to pass onto our children. We do that because we care about them and want them to be safe and to succeed. If we allow ourselves to become painfully aware of our parents' biases and prejudices, we might avoid passing on repeated patterns of survival.

> For so many of us, our parents have had regrets, disappointments, and unfulfilled dreams. From a very young age we heard them tell their stories. Through their eyes, unshed tears, silenced screams, interactions with others, and ourselves we heard their story again and again. For many of us, our parents' sad, nostalgic story of regrets, disappointments, and unfulfilled dreams became our own. For me, my parents' story was so overpowering that I was unable to learn what my own story was. Before I ventured out into life there was no space for my own regrets, disappointments, and unfulfilled dreams. There was no space for knowing what dreams I had in the first place. And, perhaps, they would not be unfulfilled—those unknown dreams!
>
> It takes energy, strength and courage for me to clear some space for myself through that learned clutter of other peoples' lives. (Journal entry 1998)

The reality is young children depend upon adults for survival in concrete ways. Children could physically live or die at their caregivers' hands. They need emotional approval and love as much, if not more than the shelter, food, and clothing adults provide. Young children try to please and imitate significant adults in their lives whom they need for their emotional and physical survival. In that way, they learn what and who is safe or dangerous.

Religious Beliefs and Practices

Bias for survival includes religious beliefs and practices. Some people feel certain that how they live and what they believe will ensure their entry to heaven. The concept of heaven differs for everyone. Belief in a higher power is an important influence on many people. Throughout the ages, religion has been the cause for many wars. People were so sure that their religious beliefs would solve the world's problems and give personal salvation to everyone that they were willing to enforce it violently. In many cases, they wanted to get rid of people in other groups rather than take them into their fold. In other cases, they felt it was worth fighting for everyone to join their group. Some use force, others persuasion.

Religious missionaries were sent out to educate indigenous groups of people whose religion was considered primitive or inappropriate. Missionaries have encouraged and convinced groups of people that what they believed or practiced was wrong or even evil. Some missionaries taught that belief in their God and adherence to religious practice would bring salvation. During the fourteenth and fifteenth centuries, my father's family fled east from the Inquisition of Spain and Portugal to North Africa, Turkey, and finally Rhodes Island, Greece. The *Marranos*, as they were known, escaped persecution and massacre in order to hold onto their Jewish faith rather than convert to Catholicism which was the decree of that time. In Rhodesia, missionaries from different parts of the Western world persuaded Native Africans (as with the Native Americans and African slaves) to convert to Christianity. This form of persuasion often did more than convert groups of people to a different religion. It was forceful and, in time, wiped out entire cultures of origin.

Living with What We Know

It is difficult to rid ourselves of emotional memories of the safe and familiar that we learned in early childhood. Sometimes we cling onto the ways of the past even though they might cause us or others pain in the present. Some people cling with certainty to what they have been taught even if they were abused. Gloria Steinem writes that change is "cold and lonely" even if it is for the better (1993, 38). She agrees that we are more able to change "old and unchosen patterns" when we become conscious of them. However, it feels unfamiliar,

> . . . as if we were out there on the edge of the universe with the wind whistling past our ears—because it does not feel *like home*. Old patterns, no matter how negative and painful they may be, have an incredible magnetic power—because they *do* feel *like home*. (38)

Alice Miller writes extensively about child abuse and cycles of violence. She describes the reluctance that adults often feel at confronting their own childhood because it is uncomfortable for them to remember what it felt like to be small, helpless children (Miller 2001). "As children, we learn to suppress and deny natural feelings and to believe sincerely that the cuffs and blows we receive are for our own good and do us no lasting injury" (121). Miller expresses concern that many adults, including teachers, believe in punishment for children because they grew up in an "atmosphere of violence" (64). If teachers are not given training that helps them understand children's suffering, they will have little awareness that "using physical force against children merely teaches them to behave aggressively later in life" or that "being subjected to physical attacks that they are unable to fend off merely instills in children a gut feeling that they do not deserve protection or respect" (64–65). Although many people believe that spanking did not harm their emotional development, they have no idea how life might have been without it. According to Alice Miller and Bruce Perry, cognitive development (or academic achievement and intelligence) is inextricably linked with early emotional experiences. In other words, the way we think and how we choose to solve problems is influenced by emotional memories.

In his book *Emotional Intelligence*, Daniel Goleman describes how bias and prejudice is developed in our childhood as a kind of "emotional learning that occurs early in life, making these reactions especially hard to eradicate entirely, even in people who as adults feel it is wrong to hold them" (1997, 156). Changing intellectual beliefs is easier than a person's deepest feelings, and even if diversity training programs might be good at raising "collective awareness . . . that bigotry and harassment are not acceptable and will not be tolerated," it is unrealistic to expect that such programs will "uproot deeply held prejudices" (159). Goleman goes on to say that this type of emotional learning can be "relearned" but that it will take time.

Relearning Bias

It is not so much our judgments as it is our prejudices that constitute our being. This is a provocative formulation, but I am using it to restore to its rightful place a positive concept of prejudice that was driven out of our linguistic usage by the French and English Enlightenment. It can be shown that the concept of prejudice did not originally have the meaning we have attached to it. Prejudices are not necessarily unjustified or erroneous, so that they inevitably distort the truth. In fact, the historicity of our existence entails that prejudices, in the literal sense of the word, constitute the initial directness of our whole ability to experience. Prejudices are biases of our openness to the world. (Gadamer 1976, 9)

A few years ago I facilitated diversity training for high school teachers where we watched a teaching video titled *The Color of Fear* (Stir Fry Productions, Oakland, CA). In a scene in the video, one of the characters says to another, "My survival affects how I hear you." In other words, my life experiences and how I have been taught to survive influences or colors the way I hear what you have to say. This statement sums up the barriers we face in communication specifically with regard to our prejudices. A young African American student poet spoke to my undergraduate class one evening. He talked about growing up in the 'hood. He described how when he walks down a street he hears the locks on white people's car doors snapping shut as they drive by him. He interprets the white people's doors locking as fear of him, an African American man. It is reasonable to suggest that sometimes he hears the locks snap shut even when it does not occur. The experience has been so intense for him as he grew up that perhaps he is unable to unhear that noise in his ears. His conclusion has become that all white people fear him, an African American man. His trust was shattered.

When we confront bias, we touch the core of a person's being. It is very personal, deep, and emotional. It is connected to significant people in our lives. Society, including media, schools, and communities, influences bias as well. However, it is especially personal and close to family members when we are very young. They taught us to discern what is good and evil, right and wrong. We remember their words even after we have grown into adults, "This is the way it's got to be. Otherwise it is very dangerous, so be careful!" They warn us of all the terrible things that may happen to us if we are not careful in our relationships with people different from us. When I ask a teacher to embrace an anti-bias curriculum, I am literally reaching deep into the core of her being to say, "change everything you were taught was safe." If we allow her to be honest she might reply, "Well, I can't just change these behaviors and feelings because I need them for my survival. I don't know right from wrong any other way. It helps me live safely. I feel familiar with it. So what you're asking me is to give up the way I survive and feel safe and that is really difficult for me, almost impossible."

Accepting differences means giving up what we know and replacing it with something new and unfamiliar. This process is difficult because most of us have been taught to fear the unknown. In fact, bias is useful to us until we choose to change it. We need not be victims of bias or fear the guilt of facing ourselves as biased. We have a choice to *relearn* it. Explaining bias and prejudice does not legitimize it. Instead it becomes understandable and, thus, easier to decide whether it is useful. Understanding that bias was taught to keep us safe is the first step toward relearning it emotionally. We open up ourselves to learn new ways when we realize that, as adults, those old childhood survival skills are not needed any longer. In fact, those old ways keep us stuck emotionally and hinder our progress. But, as Goleman suggests, it takes time and we need help and support to do this.

Activist work might not be authentic unless we challenge the feelings of discomfort that rise up to greet us on the way. We have invented the way we live and we can change it. In fact, every generation has the opportunity to choose what gets passed on to the next.

Becoming Aware of Relearnable Moments

As a white, privileged Rhodesian child I was taught in direct and subtle ways that physical affection with our black African servants was forbidden. Even though my nanny would bathe me, feed me, and tend to my emotional or physical wounds, I would not allow myself to throw my arms around her, hug or kiss her, or nestle into her lap. The white community feared interracial marriage or believed that physical distance with the black community was safest. As a young woman, I returned to Zimbabwe to spend the last days of my father's life with him when he was dying of cancer. I met my nanny, Margaret, for a reunion. We hugged and kissed and wept together. It was such a relief to finally be able to hold her close to me. In an attempt to make up for all those years of an imposed, unnatural distance, we held hands and stroked each other over and over again in the town park, as my young son played close by. We both wept uncontrollably when it was time for us to part again.

It has been a struggle to relearn my prejudices. When I was eighteen- or nineteen-years-old, I met Bill Stafford, an American Peace Corps teacher, on a train traveling from Johannesburg to Bulawayo and invited him to stay with us for a while as he passed through Rhodesia. He was on his way to work in Botswana, a neighboring country. One day he and I gave a ride to a young, black African woman who was working at a friend's home. Bill jumped out and opened the front door of the car for the woman to enter. As he did that I remember feeling amazed and ashamed both at the same time. In that moment, I realized that I had learned all black African people were expected to sit at the back of the car. Bill's behavior showed me that it was natural and polite to offer a guest the front seat of the car no matter what the color of their skin. In those days, we would feel liberal or magnanimous if we simply allowed a black African person in our car at all.

In many of my friends' homes as in mine, black African servants ate their meals separately from the white African masters and mistresses of the house. Our nanny, housekeeper, cook, and gardener would sit on the floor of the back veranda to eat a porridgelike corn meal known as *sadza*. Often I would be allowed to join their mealtime. I always felt welcomed and safe as they sat cross-legged on the floor, sharing food out of the same bowls, dipping the *sadza* into the meaty gravy and then washing their hands in a large, communal, enamel bowl that they passed around to one another. Their acceptance of me was always accompanied by delight and amusement as I would roll the *sadza* around in the palm of my hand following my nanny's instructions. They would laugh out loud in a loving and delighted manner demonstrating pleasure at me that would make me feel proud to be included.

My family would eat in a dining room at a beautifully and elaborately set table. The servants would wait in the kitchen for my mother to ring the bell so that they would know when to bring in the food or take away our used plates. In my family home or when visiting friends, I had never shared the same table with black and white

Africans together. I would visit my friend's parents, Nan and Mac Partridge, as often as they would have me while my friend was at college. Mac was the principal of a black African teacher education college he had established in 1969 with the help of the World Council of Churches. His dream was that it would become a multiracial institution in the future. In those days, the United College of Education, as it was called, was situated out in the country, in an area segregated from white suburban neighborhoods. Nan and Mac lived in a small house on the campus grounds.

Dinner with the Partridges was a unique experience unlike any other I had encountered growing up in Rhodesia. One evening, when it came time to prepare dinner I went with Nan into the kitchen where she prepared the meal together with Thiwe, the maid. I was invited to help. When the meal was ready, we all sat together at the table, Nan, Mac, Thiwe, and me! I was accustomed to servants preparing the meal in the kitchen and then standing by to wait on us when a bell was rung. The idea of everyone sharing the same table together was amazing to me. I was humbled and ashamed. More important I realized I could live my life differently than I had been taught.

I have always been grateful for those moments of realization. Each time was a deep and powerful relearning experience for me. Sometimes the smallest incidents can shock us into a deeper understanding if we allow ourselves to relearn them. It is those small behaviors that create the prejudices we learn as young children. Changing those seemingly small actions challenge the status quo, undo what we have been taught, and change the need for our bias or old survival skills. That's why, for example, Rosa Parks' action to sit at the front of the bus was so monumental. In an anthology of poems, *On the Bus with Rosa Parks*, Rita Dove writes poignantly about Parks' simple act of courage (1999, 83).

Rosa

How she sat there,
the time right inside a place
so wrong it was ready.
That trim name with
its dream of a bench
to rest on. Her sensible coat.

Doing nothing was the doing:
the clean flame of her gaze
carved by a camera flash.
How she stood up
when they bent down to retrieve
her purse. That courtesy.

Edward James Olmos is an American actor and community activist. He appeared in movies like *Selena* and *Stand and Deliver* and received an Emmy and Golden Globe award for his role in *Miami Vice*. In addition, Olmos is the U.S. Goodwill Ambassador for UNICEF. I heard Olmos address a very large group of early childhood educators at the annual conference of the California Association for the Education of Young Children (2002). His presentation focused on the role we have in helping children understand the richness of diversity in our nation. He was concerned that we should prepare children for the future by helping them appreciate diversity. More specifically, Olmos talked about a project called *Americanos: Latino Life in the United States*, which celebrated Latino culture using photography, music, film, and print. He used many interesting, humorous, and unconventional techniques so that his audience would appreciate their own diversity.

In the middle of his keynote speech, he paused and looked out at the audience. There was almost a full minute of silence before he said, "People, let me tell you something. Jesus was not white, or blonde with blue eyes!" He described the period in which Jesus lived in Jerusalem and Nazareth. Olmos talked about the fact that most likely Jesus was brown-skinned with dark, curly hair. His point was that Latino or African American people have no role models or images as important as Jesus with which to identify. According to Olmos, the white, dominant culture had decided that Jesus was white and blonde with blue eyes thereby excluding everyone else. Moreover that decision was not even based on fact or likelihood.

As he spoke I remembered a Jef Wouters' poster of a brown Madonna and child in my friend Jan's home. I was probably seventeen-years-old when I first saw it. I remembered standing very silently in front of the painting. I was aghast! By the time I was seventeen I had never thought of seeing the Madonna and child portrayed any other way than white with European and Caucasian features. My perception had been completely shaped by the images I had seen throughout my childhood. I was moved so much by that picture that I purchased it. It hung on my wall for over twenty years and, sadly, was damaged during my move to the United States. I understood exactly what Edward James Olmos was saying. He gave pride to the large Latino community who was present to hear his speech. By sharing an alternative vision of the image of Jesus, Olmos immediately included everyone. The atmosphere was emotionally intense and full of the healing pain of inclusion. I wept.

Discomfort Blocks Our Way

Recently at a national early childhood conference I gave a workshop entitled *Confronting Our Discomfort.* I was curious why people would choose to participate in a presentation that might make them feel uncomfortable, and so at the beginning of the session I asked the participants why they chose to attend the seminar. One of the attendees described that a few weeks earlier a colleague told her she was biased. She was alarmed because she always thought she had no biases. She had come to my presentation to find out if her colleague was right. At another workshop I gave to a group of community college professors, one of them said in dismay, "Somehow it seems that the more we have done to teach people to be less biased, the more we have given the message that you belong to this or that group. We categorize people and create even more bias and problems. Why do we do that?"

There are different methods we develop to not confront our discomfort. Avoidance or being color-blind is one. Teachers tell me that they do not notice colors and that all children are exactly the same. Teachers fear they will open up a Pandora's box and make children aware of bias if it is dicussed. These teachers are avoiding their discomfort. Silence is another kind of avoidance. When a teacher avoids the subject, there is nothing to discuss. However, if adults fall silent when children ask questions that make them uncomfortable, the atmosphere immediately becomes tense and unsafe. That type of silence makes a child think, "Look out! It is not a good idea to talk about this. Something bad is happening here. I am bad for being curious about it."

Denial is yet another way to avoid confronting our discomfort. A young undergraduate student born in Buffalo, New York, told me that she thought I had an accent. She was referring to my British colonial accent that I acquired from growing up in Rhodesia. "You have an accent, too." I replied. I was referring to the wide drawl that I experience from many people in Buffalo. She exclaimed, "Oh no, I don't. I was born here!" How difficult it is to feel included when I am told that I am the one who is different. For the young student, it was not about all of us as having different accents. It was about those who were different from her, or the *other*. While the innocence about her remark was delightful at the time, inherent in it was unacceptance.

As long as we avoid facing the anxiety that surrounds the subject of bias, we remain blocked and unable to accept differences in others in ways that are meaningful, respectful, and authentic. We might pay lip service to political correctness, try and do the right thing, or imagine that we are without prejudice. We do that by dealing with cultures through a tourist approach. For example, we invite people to bring their traditional foods so that we can exclaim, "Ah, how different, exotic, and interesting you are!" Or we relate stereotypically to cultures only at holiday celebrations: At Chinese New Year we all eat rice with chopsticks while wearing pointed hats; or we wear sombreros and eat tacos on Cinco de Mayo. Many teachers think they have covered Chinese and Latino cultures by celebrating just those two holidays. I always remember a Chinese student expressing indignation when a fellow American student exclaimed to her in amazement: "I never knew Chinese people ate apples! I thought you only eat rice!" And, of course, there is always that age-old phrase, "I am not intolerant. After all, some of my best friends are Jewish/black/hispanic/white/gay."

The problem is that the bias slips out unconsciously. When that happens we cannot help but treat others unfairly or disrespectfully. Very often we are not even aware that we have been behaving without respect. We are surprised when we discover we have offended someone. We even think the other person should not have been offended. After all, we wonder why are they not over whatever it is they suffered by now? The Holocaust happened over fifty years ago, or slavery happened before we were born. Blacks have lots of opportunities, why do they still insist they are being profiled?

Clearing the Way

Hearing Someone's Pain

I remember it as if it were yesterday how I felt when I went with one of my teachers and a church member into Belk's Department Store on Main Street when I was six- or seven-years-old. I was thirsty and went instinctively to drink from the nearby water fountain. I recall my teacher jerking me away in panic from the "White" water fountain, water trailing down my pinafore. It was the first thing I remembered when my sister told me that she had died in her nineties. All of her many kindnesses to me and my family never erased that moment that defined her as an adult unable or unwilling to affirm my personhood and child's fragile self-image. (Edelman 1999, 21)

Clearing the way means finding ways to confront our discomfort so that we can become more conscious of our actions. We become more able to make space in our minds and really listen to what other people have to tell us. Their stories are rich with life experiences. When we understand them, we are able to know what offends or delights, and more importantly, we learn to hear other people's pain.

Hearing someone's pain is not easy to do especially if it seems we are to blame. When guilty feelings take over, we tend to become defensive and anxious and are unable to hear what the other person is telling us about their experience. Sometimes discussions about race are difficult because African Americans have a history with slavery and pain. White Americans become defensive in the discussion because they feel ashamed about the time of slavery. I heard an African American man on a radio talk show explaining in a deeply moving way that he did not want whites to feel guilty. He wanted instead that they would understand the pain experienced by those who suffer from discrimination.

Finding ways to confront our discomfort means we become more able to understand ourselves. Then we can deal with our survival skills. We can choose not to allow our old ways of thinking to affect how we hear others. Our behaviors become more sensitive and respectful, and we become more able to treat others with dignity.

Wary of Danger

The brain's main purpose is to keep a person alive (Perry 2001). Therefore, as the young brain stores emotional memories it is more likely to retain negative words or experiences instead of positive ones to make a person wary of danger. Perry gives the example that if a child is given two or three compliments and one reprimand, she is likely to remember the reprimand. She will learn what not to do in order to survive. Think about it. You work hard in your community and are nominated for an award for your achievements. As you enter the hall to receive your award, someone remarks that you have a run in your stocking or a button is missing. Many of us would concentrate on the flaw in our clothing instead of feeling pride and joy in the moment of achievement. Negative statements for the brain means, "Look out, be on your guard and note the danger!"

Letting Down Your Guard

> What we remember of what was done to us shapes our view, molds us, sets our stance. But what we remember is past, it no longer exists, and yet we still hold on to it, live by it, surrender so much control to it. What do we become when we put down the scripts written by history and memory, when each person before us can be seen free of the cultural, or personal narrative we've inherited or devised?
>
> When we ourselves can taste that freedom? (Walker 2001, 307)

Much of relearning prejudice is about letting down your guard. I have discovered that most people have similar aspirations as me. All people have feelings that include love, hate, fear, anger, jealousy, joy, and so many more. Their way of expressing them may be different but feelings and needs are universal. People need shelter, clothes, and food as well as to be loved and acknowledged for who they are and what they do. Most people are longing for someone to listen to their life story. By letting down your guard, you become able to find the similarities of feelings and needs that bind us together as humankind.

We learn to fear sections of the community through the media. Five years after I had arrived in the United States I attended a national conference in Atlanta. I went to visit the Martin Luther King Jr. Center for Non-Violent Social Change. Martin Luther King Jr. is buried at the center. His tomb lies in a Reflection Pool with the words: "Free At Last, Free At Last, Thank God Almighty, Free At Last," inscribed on the side. Jackie and Annie, two teachers at our Child Care Center at the time, accompanied me on the field trip to the site. We were all deeply touched by the experience. On the way back to our hotel, we walked through an area that we had been warned was unsafe. What we discovered, in fact, were people walking with strollers, going into grocery stores, or standing on corners and chatting together.

Out of one of the small grocery stores, a young African American man with dreadlock curls falling about his face approached us. He asked me where we were headed and who we were. He remarked on the fact that we were carrying bags from the King Center and asked what we had learned there. I spoke enthusiastically to him about the beauty of the place and how much we had learned from visiting the site of such an important person as Dr. King. Then the man smiled and said quietly, "Well if you learned so much, why are you clutching your purse so tightly?" I looked down at my hand and saw that I was holding onto my purse with my knuckles almost white from the strain! I felt so ashamed. I could not imagine why I was behaving in that manner. There was nothing about the young man's actions that could have caused such a reaction. Personal life experiences had not caused me this kind of fear. After relaxing my grip on the purse, I apologized to the man and asked him his name. He replied, "My name is Umuali and, look, it doesn't matter. It happens all the time." Umuali walked off down one of the side streets as Jackie, Annie, and I stood still, shocked, silently as we watched him disappear.

Our field trip to the King Center had taught us much more than we imagined. We continued to walk back to the hotel through the *unsafe* neighborhood, which was nestled between luxurious conference hotels on one side, and the Martin Luther King Center on the other. I decided I had a lot of unlearning to do. Since my personal life experiences had not been the cause for such fear, I realized I must have learned about it from the media. After all, every night on the news we watch yet another story about yet another brown-skinned man who has murdered, robbed, or been drug-busted. I am grateful to Umuali for helping me identify the source of my fear. As I had learned this bias for only a brief period, I have been able to shed it quickly by letting down my guard. At the same time I understand that in our culture the fear of African American men runs deep. The earlier in our childhoods we learned this fear, the more difficult it becomes to let down our guard. Michael Moore writes:

Black men alleged to be killing, raping, mugging, stabbing, gangbanging, looting, rioting, selling drugs, pimping, ho-ing, having too many babies, dropping babies from tenement windows, fatherless, motherless, Godless, penniless. . . . No matter what city I'm in, the news is always the same, the suspect always the same unidentified black male . . . the suspect is described as a black male. . . . I believe we've become so used to this image of the black man as predator that we are forever ruined by this brainwashing. (Moore 2001, 59)

A few years ago I facilitated a support-supervision group for teachers and administrators. The purpose of the group was specifically to support early childhood professionals as they worked to implement an anti-bias curriculum in their programs. After one of the evening sessions I wrote in my journal, "After abuse and trauma, it is really difficult to let down one's guard. It is the hardest piece about survival to let go of. It is at the heart, the core, and the source of bias or prejudice." If we suffer abuse, we will develop skills to survive the experience. These skills often make us feel safe or in control of the situation. And yet in order to change biased attitudes we must learn to let down our guard, let go of the control, and learn new skills. Letting down our guard opens us up to other peoples' pain. It helps us develop a different worldview.

By now the idea of letting down your guard, releasing old patterns of survival, and changing your worldview must sound like quite a task indeed. However, while it might seem formidable it is also rewarding. It has been exciting to take charge of the way I think and feel about these things. Lately I do not feel as if I am walking through life in some unconscious dream preordained by my ancestors, family, or society. I have a conscious choice in who I become and how I behave.

What Can We Do to Clear the Way?

Admit That You Have Biases

There are things you can do to relearn prejudice and make changes to biased behaviors. First you have to admit that all of us have biases. Chances are we are all prejudiced in some way. As you admit this you will inevitably face some kind of discomfort, most likely guilt. You might think, "How could I be biased? That's awful. I don't want to think of myself as not being a nice person." We all have learned different ways of dealing with uneasy feelings because our life experiences are diverse. For some, discomfort causes anxiety, for others it might not be as painful. Remember, admitting to having biases does not legitimize unfair behaviors. Once you acknowledge your biases you are able to understand them more clearly: where they come from, how you acquired them, and in what ways they impede your progress. Then you are able to come to terms more easily with yourself and change behaviors in authentic ways.

Clearing the Way Takes Time

It is important to understand that clearing the way of discomfort takes time. There is no quick fix that rids us of bias and prejudice acquired from early childhood and adult life. We might never be able to be totally free of all our biases, but this does not mean we are unable to do effective anti-bias work. It means that we find ways to face ourselves so that we are more able to understand and negotiate our feelings of discomfort; and our behaviors or interactions become less insensitive, or offensive, or disrespectful. This process accompanies us as we do the work and supports our becoming effective agents of change.

As I write this manuscript I am watching the news closely. Senator Trent Lott, Speaker of the House, makes a speech at retiring Senator Strom Thurmond's 100th birthday party. He offends millions of Americans by insinuating that a policy of segregation would have prevented all the troubles we face today. He tries to apologize to the public and says that what he said was "repugnant . . . wicked." He tries to excuse his behavior by saying it was an "off the cuff" expression. He tells the press that if he had thought before he spoke, he might have sounded more appropriate. That is exactly how all our prejudices work. They lie in our unconscious and rise up when we least expect them. The truth about how we really feel inevitably comes out in all sorts of ways.

Education and Information

There are a number of different things we can do to help us clear our way. One of them is at a cognitive level. Education and information

makes one aware of societal prejudice. Taking courses, reading literature, and educating oneself promote cognitive self-reflection. I learned
much through reading and especially taking college courses. I am sure
we all remember professors who challenged our perceptions about
society. An inspirational teacher causes confusion and dissonance in
our current thinking, which helps expand our knowledge base and
construct new ways of understanding. I remember one course that
changed my life. It challenged my acceptance of women and men's
traditional roles in society and awakened me to feminism. How exciting that was! It opened up different possibilities for my perceptions,
most especially in the view I had about myself.

The course was about doing qualitative research. One of the required
texts was an ethnography entitled, *Educated in Romance: Women, Achievement, and College Culture* (Holland and Eisenhart 1990). The authors
explore how young women start out in college pursuing a profession
of their dreams. At a certain point they start to change their course of
studies in order to fit in with their romantic partners. Very often they
will change to a more nurturing profession, like teaching or nursing or
even give up college studies altogether in order to support their partners who want to pursue their careers. It is the age-old story where a
woman supports her husband in furthering his career at the expense
of her own. The ethnography moved me in two ways. First, I was able
to identify with the young women the authors describe. This had been
the story of my life. I had sacrificed my career to support my first husband. I was able to continue college studies only much later in my forties. Second, I was shocked because the study was written in the 1990s.
In other words, it is still going on. With all the progress women have
made, there is still a long way to go.

From that point on, I read everything I could find about feminism
past and present. The course made me aware of how few choices I felt
I had as a young woman. I had been "educated in romance." Teaching or nursing is as important if not more so, than many other careers.
However, nurturing professions become meaningful and rewarding if
we make a conscious choice to embrace them rather than feel it is the
only thing we are able to do in life. It was exciting to realize that it
does not have to be that way for young women today. All women can
choose to be educated in their own conscious choices thanks to feminist ideology.

Self-reflection Through Journals or Counseling

Clearing the way for emotional memories is more challenging. We need support for that. Writing a journal is helpful in keeping track of how biases affect our interactions with children, families, and colleagues. In my graduate course about multicultural education and anti-bias curriculum, the students were required to keep a journal. The purpose of the journal was specifically for reflecting on the biases that affected them on a daily basis. Many of the students expressed alarm at how many biases they had. They wrote about how ashamed they were as they discovered this. Some even described feeling disgust at themselves. By the end of the course, the students developed an understanding about their feelings of prejudice. They started to figure out ways to let go of biases. Writing all of this down helped them make an emotional connection to how they had learned them in the first place.

> The act of remembering is risky, painful. But once we put something into words or write it down, it doesn't seem as terrible as we felt it to be at the time. Shame and grief fester in silence. Putting things into words is what makes us human, it is what human beings do. (Chesler 2001, 28)

Journal writing is not a new tool for self-reflection. Many diet companies, fitness trainers, and authors insist that journaling about how much food a person eats during the day is one of the most effective tools for weight loss (Greene 2002). Journal writing keeps us aware of thoughts and feelings (or morsels of food!) that might otherwise slip by. Teacher-educators require students to write journals about experiences in student teaching practice. A bias awareness journal supports us as we face the feelings of shame or guilt. In private, we can keep track of difficult feelings that rise up to greet us in our anti-bias work.

For example, I watched the movie *White Man's Burden* with my students. The movie shows a reversal of our sociopolitical structure, with all the wealthy successful people depicted as black, and the inner-city population as predominantly white. I often use it in my classes to provoke discussion about racial inequality. After watching the movie one night I wrote:

Watching *White Man's Burden* this time around I became aware of my discomfort with continually seeing the "rich" and "good" guys as black. I couldn't identify with them deep down—with their kisses, concerns, wealth—as I do if they would be white. It is alarming to become aware of this. That is the major discomfort. The real prejudice—the feeling of "what's wrong with this picture?" Imagine how blacks, Asians, Hispanics, etc. must feel— no one to identify themselves with—always uncomfortable or become desensitized with seeing the other in the media. "Where am I?" "What about me?" (Journal entry 2002).

Writing a journal is effective in keeping counsel with your self. However, sometimes it is helpful to share personal feelings with a counselor. Over the years I have found support through counselors or therapists who are qualified to listen to me unconditionally. They reflect back the ways I perceive my life or the choices I have made. They give me different options and open doors for me to understand myself more clearly. Sharing difficult feelings with someone else has been effective for me in making changes in my behaviors and perceptions. It is important for me that the person I share these feelings with is not just a friend or a family member. I prefer a detached, professional person because she or he does not become involved with me on a personal level. That way, I am able to work at self-reflection without becoming bogged down in emotional involvement. I feel comfortable because it becomes more like a working relationship. The boundaries are clearer for me that way.

There are many different kinds of counselors who use a variety of strategies and methods. It takes time to develop a trusting relationship with a counselor in order to share your most personal life experiences and emotions. Many people still believe that counseling is only for people with big problems. In a society that encourages independence instead of interdependence, asking for help is often considered a weakness. Some people might feel ashamed to even entertain the thought of approaching a counselor of any kind.

Seeking support gets labeled "wimpy" in this culture when, actually, finding support and gathering the resources others have to offer is fundamental to our ability to be autonomous, to care for ourselves. (Debold, Wilson, and Malave 1993, 241)

I like to think of self-reflection and awareness as supporting me in becoming the best I can be for my family and myself, as well as in my work with the professional community. Over the years I have learned that reaching out for support is strength not weakness. I am not ashamed to ask for help in something as important as self-understanding. After all, the more I am able to understand my self, the more effective I will be in understanding others. Remember, "My survival affects how I hear you," from earlier in this chapter? Well, I hear you more clearly when I free myself from old survival scripts that block our communication.

Working alone with a counselor is less private than writing in a journal. Learning to understand oneself and others can also be effective within a support group. In a support group setting, you hear others working through their issues while sharing yours. There is support through hearing about similarities. It helps to know that others are experiencing similar types of discomfort. At the same time, you learn about the differences of each participant of the group: how they solve problems; acquired their belief system; learned to express emotions; developed biases; what causes them emotional pain; and so on. In Chapter 5 I share with you how I set up a support group for teachers that was specific to confronting discomfort about bias.

We Need Support to Face Discomfort

Anti-bias work is crucial in early childhood. Children can become prejudiced by age two. We have an awesome responsibility as early childhood teachers and, as Bruce Perry says, "early childhood is the easiest time to create humane people" (Perry 2002). However, because the subject affects us in deeply emotional ways, our discomfort associated with bias is often unbearable and we need support to face it. Teaching can be a lonely profession. Teachers make moment-to-moment decisions in their interactions alone with children. Some of these interactions affect children for the rest of their lives.

> It is true, of course, that no teacher is an island, none is a perfectly free agent. Teachers are shaped by powerful social and economic forces, forces that coerce and constrain, prod and bombard, push and pull. Teachers are particularly formed by

their relationships to power and their role in a bureaucracy geared to reproducing the social relations of society.

But it is also true that teachers finally decide what goes on in classrooms. When the door is closed and the noise from outside and inside has settled, the teacher chooses. . . . There are all kinds of ways to choose, all kinds of ways for people to invent their teaching in a world that is often resistant and problematic. (Ayers 1991, 48)

In and Out of Confidence

I worshipped dead men for their strength,
Forgetting I was strong.

Vita Sackville-West, in Steinem, *Revolution from Within*

Once we are old enough to have had an education, the
first step toward self-esteem for most of us is not to learn
but unlearn. *We need to demystify the forces that have*
told us what we should be *before we can value what we*
are.

Gloria Steinem, *Revolution from Within*

At the end of the day, one of the mothers of a child in our center ran breathlessly in to pick up her daughter. I was in the front lobby working at our copy machine. The woman came up to me puffing and panting as if she had been running, her eyes were wide with excitement. She waved her hand in the air and said, "What's that expression you use? The one you'll use for your book, the one you write about? That confidence thing?" I smiled and suggested, "In and out of confidence?" "Yes!" she exclaimed, "That's the one! Well I am in confidence right now and that's pretty dangerous I can tell you." "Hmm . . . dangerous, eh?" I replied. "Yes!" she almost shouted. "I can move mountains and change the world when I feel like this." Two other women walked by to pick up their children. They stopped close to us, smiled and nodded. They understood. I hugged her. I said, "That's a wonderful feeling. How interesting, though, that it feels dangerous to you. Enjoy it! Relish it! Don't feel guilty for it." Everyone laughed out loud and as they walked to the classrooms to pick up their children they talked to each other animatedly about feeling "in confidence."

I thought about that mother and the women who agreed with her. They are not early childhood professionals. All three work in completely different fields. However, they all identified with a feeling of danger about being in confidence. Surely feeling strong and assertive should be exciting. I wondered if men feel dangerous when they are in confidence or whether they allow themselves to feel exhilarated and excited about it. I thought about women who are taught to be demure, shy, or quiet. Or how we say to little girls that they are pretty or cute. Are we excited when they are strong and competent as we are with little boys? Do we even expect girls to be strong and assertive?

For a few years now I have been writing a newsletter column titled *In and Out of Confidence* for our local Association for the Education of Young Children (AEYC). The title came to me one morning, when I was experiencing some confusion about myself. I was expressing this confusion to Tom, my husband, as I called out, "Oh no, today is not going to be easy. I don't know if I am in or out of confidence!"

So, I started by writing the newsletter column. It has been an excellent boost for my feelings of *in confidence*. Many people have given me feedback in all sorts of ways. Some have disagreed with my opinions and have taken the trouble to give me a call or write a note. Others have been grateful because my stories have been a reflection of their own feelings. Mostly, there has been an excited response from many people in our early childhood community, who are delighted to know that I feel the way they do. In one article I wrote:

We talk and talk about *self-esteem*. Hardly any of us know what self-esteem is. We might define, read, or think about it. But how many of us really know what it feels like to be confident, strong, and aware of what we are capable of; or to be proud and passionate about our potential strengths? How many of us fearlessly stand up for what we believe in and fight for our principles with all our might and mane? Very few, I suspect. We have no notion of what self-esteem feels, tastes, smells, or sounds like. Who can know? We were taught from very early on that silliness and smiley faces were cute and that our feelings and thoughts were not respected. When, as teachers, our walls are plastered with care bears and clowns, silly, smiling animals and bubbles and balloons? Who can know? Children are trivialized until they can no longer feel. Their emotions become numb and they grow into adults who are out of touch with their feelings.

If or how you fight for children is connected with how you feel about yourself, how you were related to as a child, and how you relate to your inner child presently. Who helps you identify all these emotions, relationships, and connections? I have journeyed through therapy much of my professional life. On my journey, I have met a number of therapists. All have different theories and styles. As I reflect now, I realize that at each stage I chose different people who guided me in different ways. With each person I was willing to open up to my inner self a fraction more. It has been intriguing, as I delved into the depths of my emotions and relationships and began to make connections about why I do what I do and where my behaviors, interactions, thoughts, feelings, fears, and joys come from.

Our inner life is almost like the unraveling of a mystery novel. Engaging with our inner child and confronting our fears is painful and uncomfortable but a relief at the same time. Somehow we grow more confident and are able to change why we do what we do. (Meyer November/December 1998)

Being *In and Out of Confidence* Is About Self-Esteem

Our authentic identification depends on our core feelings and self-appraisals. (Person 2002, 43)

It is my contention that many teachers of young children and those who choose early childhood education as a profession tend to suffer from low self-esteem. This is serious with regards to how it might affect our relationships with children and families. We must face ourselves on a personal level and as a profession in terms of how we feel our worth is judged by society. Being *in and out of confidence* is about self-esteem.

Gloria Steinem shares the view that outside forces have an enormous impact on how we develop a sense of ourselves (1993). In *Revolution from Within: A Book of Self-Esteem* she makes connections between how we were raised as young children and how we see ourselves as adults. "To put it another way: I began to understand that self-esteem isn't everything; it's just that there's nothing without it" (26). Like Steinem, I am drawn to the subject of self-esteem "not only because other people needed it, but because I did" and "my image of myself was very distant from other people's image of me; and that, in short, my childhood years . . . [are] still shaping the present as surely as a concealed magnet shapes metal dust" (6–7).

Society Affects Our Self-Esteem

Women Are Not Taken Seriously

Society—a web of many patriarchal families, both nuclear and extended—does not always welcome all women. (Chesler 2001, 13)

Self-esteem of teachers of young children is affected by two social systems. The first relates to the fact that early childhood education professionals are predominantly women. There are very few men who work in early care and education programs. At our annual national association conference of more than twenty thousand educators each year, probably no more than 5 percent of the attendees are men. Many of my colleagues joke about the men's restrooms. They say that they might as well be taken over by us, as convention centers never seem prepared for that amount of women all at once. After the first day, women post handwritten "Women" signs on the men's restroom doors. A tiny revolution occurs because of our restroom needs. Women take charge. Their signs make a statement, "Don't you realize that early childhood means lots of women? Relate to our needs!"

As we discussed in Chapter 2, societal systems affect our biases. Women's sense of self-worth is affected by patriarchy, which is structured by principles of power, dominance, and control. From a system like that we learn not to trust ourselves or our abilities. In fact, some of us learn, like the mother in the childcare center, that it is dangerous even to feel powerful. Racism and sexism (pieces of patriarchy) are "thieves of self-esteem" (Steinem 1993). We have been raised to assume that power comes from outside of ourselves, and powerful people, usually men, are the givers of approval. "Patriarchy, racism, class systems . . . ration self-esteem . . . create obedience to external authority by weakening belief in our natural and internal wisdom" (33).

Many girls today are encouraged to be ambitious and realize their professional aspirations. While there have been concrete changes in the

everyday lives of women and men that offer women many more opportunities, something still seems to hold "women back from a run for
the roses" (Person 2002). "Our lingering gender stereotypes persist, as
do the value judgments with which we rationalize them" (236). Author
bell hooks describes patriarchy as affecting men and women in that we
all are capable of acting in oppressive ways (hooks 2000b). She reminds
us that we need to resist an oppressor that we have internalized.

When I came to the United States in my late thirties I only had a
preschool teacher credential, which I earned from the Israeli Ministry
of Education in the early 1970s. I was full of determination and excitement at the opportunity to finally realize my dream of acquiring
a higher education. At the same time I felt anxious and uncertain
about my intellectual or scholarly abilities. Quite honestly, I was terrified. When I think back about my arrival in the United States and
the university community, I am sometimes ashamed at how naïve and
innocent I actually was. I entered a territory that I had been socialized to believe belonged to the world of men: academia-land. While
I felt grateful to be allowed in I had no life experience that helped me
develop the skills needed to negotiate it. In my department there was
no mentor other than my major advisor. As I progressed through my
studies and work as adjunct faculty, I discovered that my anxiety about
academia-land was not unrealistic or naïve. Some of my worst fears
were realized.

At first I received encouragement and support from my major advisor who also posed as a friend. Very soon I began to discover that
his relationship and interactions with me had little to do with my
academic ability or interests, and more to do with sexual attraction
and emotional intimacy. For a short while it seemed flattering, however, my higher education was leading me into a realm of feminist
awareness that I had not achieved in the years prior to this. I began
to set boundaries and request respect for my intellectual interests. Very
quickly the situation became unbearable. I realized with horror that
I was on the brink of being forced out of his/our department. I had
become a victim of sexual harassment.

After resigning my position and changing advisors, I appealed for
help through every appropriate channel I could find in the department
and university. I got nowhere. It was not just the man, the system as
a whole protected the man. People high up in the administration of

our school immediately questioned my motives in stereotypical ways. One person called me a "bitch," and yet another suggested that I was reacting out of jealousy toward other women students favored by my advisor. It was almost impossible to be taken seriously. Those who did remained silent. Since then, I have faced occasional though notable barriers to professional advancement within the academic system of the university due to my speaking out. It took six years before the university organized a sexual harassment policy. It was too late for me.

That incident served as my initiation into the academic system. It took a huge emotional toll on me as well as almost jeopardizing my professional progress. Throughout the experience, I felt devastated and learned a great deal about my own self-worth as I staggered in and out of confidence. At first, I felt guilt about causing trouble for my "friend" and the university community. Then I felt shame that I had not established clear boundaries from the outset. As I processed and confronted these painful feelings I realized how much I had been socialized to devalue my intellectual worth over sexual attractiveness. I had been truly educated in romance. In the most painful way possible I began to un-learn the way I had been taught to value myself in the past. At the deepest level of my self-esteem I understood what Steinem meant by patriarchy creating "obedience to external authority by weakening belief in our natural and internal wisdom" (1993, 33). Many women, both faculty and students, experience what I did. It is not only students and faculty. It is other women everywhere.

Thanks to the support and friendship from one or two women in the community, I was able to survive the experience. I came out of it stronger than ever. It has made me acutely aware of and sensitive to the challenges that women face within a system that still values sexual attractiveness over strength and intellectual ability. At every level of society, we still have a long way to go to ensure that we are taken seriously and are treated with respect.

Our Profession Is Not Taken Seriously

Our work positions us in a social hierarchy. The prestige and recognition accorded to different jobs depends on current social attitudes. (Person 2002, 239)

A second social force that affects early childhood teachers' self-esteem is that society considers our profession low on the totem pole. Child-care and education are feminist issues. We have been socialized to believe that women not only should take care of children, but that they all love to do so. And, they love it so much that they seem willing to do it for free or close to it. At every level of our professional lattice I hear early childhood educators declare, "I don't do this for the money. It's because I love children!" Many people seem to perceive us as just a bunch of women watching a bunch of kids. Because of this overwhelming societal view that early childhood educators (mostly women) are no more than babysitters, many states across the nation do not require teachers in child care and education programs to have credentials higher than a high school diploma. Early childhood teachers receive some of the lowest compensation for their work. Many receive no health or retirement benefits or paid sick time. In other words, women's work in this field is not taken seriously.

When money is used as one of the chief criteria for determining an individual's success, it is likely to result in the judging of value of certain professions, as well as the level of success an individual has achieved. Therefore, if we were to compare required educational credentials and salaries for doctors and lawyers, for example, with those of early childhood professionals, a clear statement is made. According to our monetary/societal system, people who care for and educate children are less valuable. In fact, in some states teachers in childcare settings are paid less than garbage collectors or parking attendants. This cannot help but create feelings of low self-worth. While we might not think we do this work for the money, financial compensation plays a role in determining who we are!

Many early childhood professionals feel marginalized or victimized. Lack of self-esteem is reinforced and confirmed at every level of society. Wherever I travel, I see women who are intelligent, courageous, and valuable, who do not think they are. So much of my work is with teachers who work directly with children and families of childcare and education programs. Most of the women I meet experience societal barriers, which reinforce their feelings of low self-esteem no matter how competent they are.

Everybody's paid but teacher
Carpenter, mason, and clerk;
Everybody's paid but teacher,
She gets nothing but work.
Everybody's paid but teacher,
Toiling day and night;
Everybody's paid but teacher,
Butcher, baker, and cook;
Everybody's paid but teacher,
Grafter, fakir, and crook.
Everybody's paid but teacher,
Paid with a scowl or smile;
Everybody's paid but teacher,
Whose work is not worthwhile.
Everybody's paid but teacher,
Seeking her pay above;
Everybody's paid but teacher,
Living on ethereal love.

(*Harris 1906*)

This poem opens a book about the history of American women teachers (Carter 2002). While the book covers important topics of rights for female teachers like equal pay for equal work or the right to lobby and bargain collectively, there is no mention of the plight of early childhood education teachers. Most of the discussion is about teachers in elementary and higher education. Our early care and educators do not feature in the history of American women teachers. There are no unions to protect us. "Our childcare providers are among the lowest earners among all workers, with an average salary of just $15,430 per year" (Robinson and Stark 2002, 1).

Staff turnover in childcare centers has reached crisis proportions. One of the main reasons is low compensation for teachers who have achieved college degrees. It seems that even as we assume that all women love to work for free when taking care of children, somehow they still need money to survive.

If we have low self-esteem it is difficult to respect ourselves because we do not feel deserving of respect. If we have little faith in our own intrinsic worth, we are likely to expect that we will not be taken seriously. Respecting others or taking them seriously is one of the most fundamental requirements for accepting diversity. When we value others we become able to hear their pain and thus treat them with respect. These qualities are intrinsic to anti-bias activist work. If we do not feel respect for ourselves and accept our shortcomings, how do we respect others? One of the hardest most abstract aspects of emotional development is our capacity to value the self (Perry 2001).

Early Childhood Education Is an Important and Rewarding Career
I do not want the reader to think for one moment that I devalue the profession of early childhood education. For three decades I have worked with children, families, and teachers of young children. Indeed, I believe it to be the most important and rewarding profession in the world. Certainly recent brain development research has confirmed and reinforced the importance of the first years of life, and thus our role in improving the quality of care and education.

But that is not the only reason I value this profession so highly. I think of how one of the head teacher's eyes fill with tears of passion, pride, and love when she talks about the work she does with our youngest children at the University Child Care Center. She laughs at people who say to her, "Oh, so you just sit and rock babies in your lap all day?" She replies, with fire in her eyes, "Give me babies to rock all day! How lucky I am! Oh my goodness, rocking babies is the most important thing I could ever do!" This woman cherishes each moment she has with children. She studies, reads, and develops herself professionally so that she can give the best care and education to every child who comes into her classroom. She understands that she will affect those children for the rest of their lives. She is convinced that it is the most important and rewarding career she could have chosen.

There are many of us who feel passion and commitment to the profession. We have enormous pride and satisfaction in the work we do even though it is during long hours every day, all year round for very little pay. We know we are making a difference in improving quality of life for our youngest children. By the love we give out daily in this work we are activists and advocates for excellence in care and education. However, even those dedicated teachers are called "just babysitters" over and over again. I observe the hurt and anger they feel when that happens. I feel it too. They must surely feel confused about the importance of their work when they open a paycheck only to realize that they will have to take on one, perhaps two, additional jobs to make ends meet.

Since I came to the United States over a decade ago, I completed three degrees (BA, Master's and Ph.D.) in early childhood education. I am adjunct faculty at the university and participate in many organizations in the community and at the state level doing advocacy work for children and families. In addition, I present extensively about diversity and appropriate practices. However, when I attend parties with university faculty (men or women) from different departments, or people from the corporate and business sectors (women or men), their conversation with me ceases the instant I say that I am a director of a child care center. Their eyes glaze over and often they turn away to talk with someone else. There is no interest in that part of my work. When that happens, my self-esteem starts to slide downward and I feel despairing and lonely. Despairing and lonely is about what happens inside of me. In fact, I feel angry. Anger is about what happens outside of me. In other words, as I start to experience the discomfort of anger, I internalize it and feel bad about myself instead.

Self-Esteem and Anger

> Not all negative feelings diminish our sense of power. Rage, resentment, anger, fury, jealousy, and envy are feelings often connected with action, assertion, and the exertion of one or another kind of power. They propel us to right the wrongs we have suffered and to fight on our own behalf. (Person 2002, 39)

Feelings of low self-worth are usually accompanied by anger and resentment. These are some of the most uncomfortable emotions we face. Significant adults in our lives taught us that anger is a bad and dangerous feeling. From about eighteen-months-old, children are taught that they are unacceptable if they show anger. Young children are punished and dealt behavior modifications for tantrums and other angry outbursts from the moment they say, "No!" How we rush to suppress children's expression of anger!

It is important that we help children understand that we want them to be safe and protected by the necessary rules that benefit all citizens of a democratic society. However, much of adults' discomfort around children's expression of anger is about obedience and control. Anger is an important emotion. It is normal for all human beings to feel angry. That is when they realize their rights are being violated. Anger serves as a warning for self-protection. It can be a productive emotion. It is the agent that inspires people to fight for civil rights. Anger helps us say, "Hey, you are standing on me! That hurts! Please get off me! I don't like it when you do that (or say those things) to me! I have the right to fair treatment—to dignity!"

Feelings of anger are not bad or dangerous. Children are not evil if they feel anger. Our role is to guide children toward appropriate expression of anger. Our responsibility is to help them feel safe and acceptable for having uncomfortable feelings. We are teachers and caregivers, not state wardens. However, mostly we punish children and make them feel bad for even feeling angry in the first place. We say things like, "That's not nice. Don't be angry. Be nice to that person, go hug them." If a child continues to experience anger after being told to stop, she learns there is something wrong with her for feeling it in the first place. Instead of understanding strong emotions and learning how to monitor anger, children will most likely push uncomfortable feelings into some dark, deep place within their unconscious. As adults we sometimes become unable to feel or understand our emotions at all. These feelings have become unconscious. Anger becomes unacceptable to us.

We are taught from an early age to obey authority mostly without question. Teachers may call it, "Following orders." Girls tend to be socialized to be good, sweet, caring, and demure. Anger is usually even more unacceptable for girls than boys. Women are called derogatory names for assertive behavior or expressions of anger. The word "bitch" comes to mind. As I write this I recall the images we see of women in the Middle East under oppressive *burkha*s silently suffering unfair treatment without an outlet for any of the anger they might feel. It is all just a matter of degree, isn't it? Anger and resentment become part of a whole package of feeling undeserving and worthless that is connected to low self-esteem. "Power is experienced as exhilarating and is connected to pride, but powerlessness . . . is connected to feelings of humiliation and shame" (Person 2002, 46).

How Do We Deal with Uncomfortable Feelings?

"The unfolding research on the brain is unequivocal testimony to the fact that the future of any community literally rests on the laps of those who nurture its youngest members" (Karr-Morse and Wiley 1997, 297). Here is precisely where the political links with the personal. Early childhood educators have an enormous responsibility. In *Ghosts from the Nursery: Tracing the Roots of Violence*, Karr-Morse and Wiley explain how early emotional learning with significant adults in children's lives, including parents and early childhood educators, affects children's ability to learn abstract concepts. "As the result of early emotional learning, we tend to replicate familiar relationship patterns and confirm the view we formed early how relationships work" (184). Academic success and cognitive development depends on successful attachment, guidance in expressing difficult emotions, and trusting relationships.

> When children have not been able to achieve some level of trust in at least one other person, when they are coming to school or to play groups with strong feelings of fear, rage or grief learning is compromised. The ability to focus on abstract concepts requires some degree of emotional security. (Karr-Morse and Wiley 1997, 202)

Both Gloria Steinem and Germaine Greer use the expression "the political is personal" (Greer 1999, Steinem 1993). They mean it in the context of awareness of the sociopolitical culture of oppression as it affects one's inner life, relationships, and behaviors. Children need teachers to help them develop attachment and trust. They depend on their teachers to support difficult emotions and guide them in appropriate expressions of their feelings. In 1998, 73 percent of mothers with children one year or older were employed with 52 percent working full-time (Robinson and Stark 2002). For much of the year, day in and day out, children in early childhood programs rely on teachers and caregivers to help them learn to be respectful of others.

What are we doing, if anything, for those teachers who are unable or afraid to confront feelings of low self-esteem, anger, and resentment? Like all biases, or survival skills learned in childhood, unconscious emotions determine our behaviors and interactions. Indeed much of the anger or resentment we might be feeling is acquired from families and communities who devalue what we do and who we are.

> Feelings tell us different things about ourselves. They help us scan the inner and outer worlds, prodding both self-knowledge and knowledge of the outside world. Being in touch with our feelings is one of the primary ways we can navigate through our lives. Just as important, feelings are instruments of our global self-evaluations, telling us how we're doing, mediating our sense of power or powerlessness, our experience of ourselves as weak or strong. Alerted to feelings of weakness, we are sometimes able to change course and avoid a downward spiral. But sometimes we can be so overwhelmed by almost exactly the same feelings that we become paralyzed—incapacitated and powerless. (Person 2002, 39)

I worry about how those teachers with low self-esteem deal with uncomfortable feelings during all those hours alone with young children. How are they able to value children and families when they do not feel valued themselves? How can teachers support children's self-identity with integrity and dignity when they lack confidence, or when they feel unworthy and undeserving of fair treatment themselves? Who will help them unpack and understand those complicated and uncomfortable feelings? And, finally, how can we expect these same teachers to implement an activist anti-bias, multicultural curriculum in early childhood programs without any emotional support for themselves?

In *Woman's Inhumanity to Woman*, Phyillis Chesler says that while she still believes in the importance of political struggle it takes a long time for "political-social programming to change human nature" (Chesler 2001). She writes: "However, I am now more realistic about how long such struggles may take and more anxious therefore that individual women work every day to strengthen and support each other while they are working to improve woman's fate during the next millennium" (17). As a woman and an early childhood educator, I work with the feelings of low self-worth every day of my life. However, when I receive support to confront some of these feelings, I am able to change my attitude. If we make changes in how we perceive our work, we will change the system.

What We Can Do to Improve Our Self-Esteem

Supportive Relationships

> Recognition is not something we seek simply to please our vanity. Recognition—confirmation, validation—is something that we require at all stages of our lives. We all need someone who knows us to endorse us as a valuable person. (Person 2002, 283)

During my adolescent years I developed relationships with two significant women, both mothers of girlfriends of mine (the first was Nan Partridge, mentioned in the previous chapter). They opened a window of intellectual opportunity for me and helped me feel worthwhile. They did this by the way they related to me. I felt worthy of their attention and humbled by their belief in my intellectual ability. They opened my eyes to the notion that women can be as strong and intelligent as men. They planted a seed that would grow and bloom later in my life. Because I was still weighed down by feelings of low self-esteem, it would take me until I was in my forties to understand what they gave me in my late teens.

I have already described how I came about feeling alienated and unworthy growing up in my family. However, being Jewish and caring about black Africans in Rhodesia earned me many enemies among my peers as well. I would find swastikas carved into my school desk. The neighborhood we lived in and schools I attended were predominantly white and racist. Most of the white Rhodesian community was racist. I spent most of my years at school anxiously trying to fit into groups that would not have me. On the other hand, I preferred to spend long hours alone because so many of my schoolmates talked and behaved in ways I could not identify with.

My sense of belonging was challenged in all the areas of my life. And as it was challenged I internalized a feeling that something must be wrong with me. My hair was too curly to fit into the straight, blonde Aryan-type model of my accepted and popular peers. I was too Jewish, although I remember being told time and again that I was "fortunate" because my nose did not "look Jewish." I was sixteen when I began to meet people who were Jewish (with the curly hair and all) or who believed that we should treat all human beings equally. I found organizations outside of my school and neighbor-hood despite the fact that I was experiencing strong feelings of low self-worth.

The second woman, Inge Wallerstein, saved my emotional life. She seemed to sense my feelings of worthlessness and lack of belonging. She affected me because she was one of the first people I remember who helped me feel worthwhile and loveable. Not only would she pamper me with treats and physical affection, she would engage me in conversations about what I was thinking and feeling about all as-pects of my life. She made the time to find out about me and seemed interested in my opinions.

She was one of the first adults in my life who related to my intel-lect. I began to feel more confident in myself because my intelligence was welcomed and valued. Inge keyed me into the idea that educa-tion is important for women as well as men. I had learned that edu-cation was important. However, it seemed to me that academic success belonged to the world of men, and specifically to my older brother. This was reinforced later in my first marriage when I was strongly encouraged by both our families to support my husband's studies by forfeiting mine. Both Inge and Nan shared their intellectual aspira-tions with me, and showed genuine interest in what I thought about social issues.

We become empowered when we reach out for support. It is never too late! I realized that reaching out to Inge and Nan had been a cou-rageous act. I had always felt that I betrayed my own mother in some way. However, when I read *Mother Daughter Revolution* and as I look back at that time in my life I am proud that I had the strength to seek out what the authors term, *othermothers* (Debold, Malave, and Wilson 1993). Significant "other" women in young girls' lives are important not only for their emotional development, but also as support for mothers. The authors describe mothering in the structure of nuclear families as exhausting and isolating in any case. They suggest that if mothers could reach out and share the burden they might "transform motherhood into a revolutionary network" (236). Certainly my own mother's life was fraught with chaos and anxiety that was emotion-ally draining. She simply did not have the emotional energy for what I needed at the time. Sometimes young girls will reach out to othermothers when they feel that their ideas might be too risky to share with their own mothers.

> Othermothers provide girls with more strategies for resistance. Othermothers, caring adults living outside the family story, love girls by choice, bring fresh eyes to the mother daughter relationship, and teach voice by embodying different ways of being women than a daughter has available in her mother. Through close relationships with othermothers, girls come to know a range of options for their lives and so experience greater control in their own lives. (237)

Inge and Nan were my othermothers. At a certain time in my life, I needed the care and education they offered me so generously. Their relationship with me sustained and gave me the hope and strength I needed to convert feelings of exclusion and worthlessness into skills necessary for acceptance of others in future anti-bias activist work. The seeds of my intellectual worth and the importance of education were planted. There have been other kinds of supportive relationships along the way with teachers, friends, or mentors. The trick for becoming more confident is in realizing that I had the strength and courage to reach out for support even as an adolescent, even when it seemed like betrayal to those close to me.

One of the ways we work at unlearning how we are valued is with the support of "othermothers and fathers" during our life. It is important to seek out those who believe in your worth and accept you unconditionally. It is hard to develop a strong sense of self when you are constantly being judged or criticized. Now that I am a teacher educator I am often sought out by students or teaching staff to be a mentor for them. After class one evening, one of the students came up to me and asked me directly, "Will you be my mentor?" I agreed instantly. "How should I do that?" I asked in reply. She looked me straight in the eye and said, "I want to just be around you, ask you questions, feel your presence, and learn from you." When someone asks you to be their mentor they probably need it! I always agree. However, it is important that you ask them, "How should I do that?" Everyone has different needs for support. Some want knowledge, others want to observe your behavior, and still others want you to listen to their ideas without judgment.

Education

"We will never, never, never, never have quality care without professional development" (Kagan 1998).

Furthering one's education is crucial for improving self-esteem. Time and again I observe women in the field of care and education becoming uplifted and confident when they take college courses or complete the Child Development Associate (CDA) credential. I will never forget the feelings I had after completing a comprehensive examination as part of the requirements for my doctorate. For eight hours I sat alone in a room writing everything I had learned about early childhood education that would show my understanding of theory and practice in the field. I was given half an hour for lunch. At the end of the exam I had written twenty-five pages.

After handing in my work I sat in my car facing the steering wheel for what seemed like an eternity. It is almost impossible to describe my sense of achievement and pride in what I had accomplished at that moment. I felt as if my heart would burst. My feelings were accompanied by disbelief that I could ever have accomplished something like that. I wept with joy and amazement at myself. Each time I hear someone declare they are unable or afraid to continue their education I try to share those feelings I had that day. Education is more than acquiring knowledge. It gives us a sense of who we are and what we are able to achieve. It allows us a deeper understanding of ourselves, which is crucial for supporting us in appropriate practice. It gives us professional competence and credibility. We become confident at a personal level.

With education we give ourselves options. We open doors that have been locked by our imagination or self-perceptions. The less ignorant we are the less we fear the unknown. Education helps us become professional. Knowledge about child development supports our appropriate practices for young children. Knowledge about ethical behavior with children, families, and colleagues shapes our decisions in every interaction. The most important role of the teacher is that of decision maker. Indeed, each decision a teacher makes should be intentional. Why we do what we do matters at every moment in the day as we work with children.

Most of my personal, emotional struggle as I completed my degrees was believing that I could do it. I would move in and out of confidence from day to day, month to month, and year to year. I needed others to believe in me. Encouragement from colleagues, my supervisor in Israel, and one or two college professors gave me hope through some dark tormented hours and helped me to develop trust in my ability and potential. As I began to find my professional voice in written papers and oral presentations, I discovered that the more I was able to support my beliefs and experiences with formal knowledge and research, the more I understood fundamentally why I do what I do. I started to feel in confidence for longer periods of time.

Over a decade ago I was first hired as the Program Coordinator at the University at Buffalo Child Care Center. The director at the time informed me that the staff was resistant to change and professional growth. I looked into the eyes of some of those women and saw myself. I believed in their practical knowledge and the skills they had developed over the years. I felt strongly that they did want to find their professional voice and be supported in their understanding of why they do what they do. Over the years, the staff has grown and grown. They read, study, and often struggle with the high standards that they now choose to uphold for themselves. Some have chosen to complete the CDA credential, and BA or Master's degrees in early childhood education. They assist in training interns who come to our center from a number of colleges in the area. Several of them present at local, state, and national conferences as well as facilitate trainings for other childcare staff in the community.

Early childhood teachers need people to believe in them and trust their ability and potential. By people I mean directors, administrators, Boards and Advisory Committees, legislators, and teacher-educators. We can show our trust by fighting for the resources to assist in professional development. If we want teachers to trust the abilities and potential of all young children, we surely must treat teachers in the same way. Supporting education of early educators is one way of ensuring fair treatment and the development of self-identity for children. Support should be ongoing through supervision, mentoring, and support groups where teachers are understood and guided through their personal journeys in and out of confidence.

We must insist that all teachers of young children become credentialed, licensed and professional. Not only will it benefit children, it will place us solidly in confidence as individuals and as a profession.

Raising the bar in education will eventually lead to higher compensation.

Self-Work as Advocacy

> All books about revolutions . . . should begin with a psychological chapter—one that shows how a harassed terrified man suddenly breaks his terror, stops being afraid. This unusual process—sometimes accomplished in an instant, like a shock—demands to be illustrated. Man gets rid of fear and feels free. Without that, there would be no revolution. (Kapuscinski, from Steinem 1993, 25)

Low self-esteem is a lonely feeling. Loneliness brings on fear, which paralyzes and renders us helpless. We allow ourselves to become victims of outside forces and learn to believe that we are unworthy or undeserving of improving our situation. It is almost as if, as I used to feel, that a type of unlucky star hangs over our heads. We need support to explore this complex area of discomfort. While it definitely helps to have a mentor, supervisor, or friend who believes in you, it is even more helpful to have a group of people supporting you through this type of difficult or painful self-reflection.

In *All About Love: New Visions,* author bell hooks suggests that reflection is useful for people who choose to "stop listening to negative voices, within and outside the self, that constantly reject and devalue them" (2000a, 56). She describes negative thinking as "absolutely disenabling" (57). When we replace it with a positive voice, writes hooks, "we not only accept and affirm ourselves, we are able to accept and affirm others" and become better prepared to take responsibility (57). We will not be able to prevent discrimination. However, "we can choose how we respond to acts of injustice. Taking responsibility means that in the face of barriers we still have the capacity to invent our lives, to shape our destinies in ways that maximize our well-being" (57). In hooks' personal journal of affirmations that she used to make changes in her own attitude she wrote: "I'm breaking with old patterns and moving forward with my life" (56). Taking responsibility means choosing to break old patterns of survival.

We gather strength with a community of people as we learn to feel valuable and worthwhile. In the following chapter, I tell about facilitating a women's support group. Some of the feelings of anger, resentment, loneliness, and fear that I mentioned earlier in this chapter were experienced during the group sessions. The good news is as we uncovered these feelings we became empowered. The women's confidence was strengthened. Some of them made concrete changes in educational practice as well as in their personal lives. Although we did not talk about in and out of confidence per se, I came to understand that it is one of our discomfort areas in the field of early childhood education.

The more we learn to understand the needs of our inner child as we were growing up, the more we become able to identify our sense of worth. Realizing that we have worth is fundamental to developing self-identity. All young children need to feel valuable as well. We must take the responsibility to be strong and confident for them. Children depend on us for guidance as they develop their self-identity or learn about expressing difficult emotions. I want our profession to be full of people who have consciously chosen to be there. I want early childhood teachers to understand that their profession is the most important in the world and that they are as valuable, or even more so, than lawyers and doctors! Young children deserve that from us.

But we cannot do this alone. The whole community, all of society, and our governments must understand this as well. Relearning a new way of perceiving ourselves is too difficult to do alone. And why should we? The patriarchal "I can do it alone, independently" model is not good for anyone, men, women, or children. Interdependence begins the moment we have the courage to reach out for support. The entire community is strengthened when we do it together.

Participation in Organizations

> Recognition and respect in one's profession often gives one the power to right a wrong, help a disadvantaged group, or correct an injustice. (Person 2002, 290)

If ever you feel out of confidence about this profession that you have chosen, attend a NAEYC conference. Each time I join the tens of thousands who attend these conferences I have the feeling that I belong to the most important profession in the world. What a huge support group! Some years there are over thirty thousand attendees from all over the nation and world.

There are a number of organizations that advocate for quality care and education as well as improving the status of teachers of young children including professional development and compensation issues. These include NAEYC, Association for Childhood Education International (ACEI), and Children's Defense Fund (CDF) to mention just a few.

You can participate in many different ways as an advocate. In *Advocates in Action*, Robinson and Stark (2002) identify different forms and levels of advocacy including leaders, advisors, researchers, contributors, and friends. As a leader you will share your vision and speak out on behalf of children and families. Serving on boards and committees, organizing conferences, and the day-to-day volunteering in organizations makes you a hard-working contributor. Attending conferences and reading professional journals keeps you aware of current ideas and practices and supports the work that you do in the field. Sharing your expertise as an advisor or consultant is an excellent way to advocate for our profession. Researchers do the crucial work of collecting and analyzing important data that will support the *why* behind *what* we do day to day with children and families. As a friend and advocate we can always donate monies to organizations, which are mostly nonprofit and need our support for the important work they do.

Anyone can join and participate in organizations. This type of participation binds us to the issues that affect us and the children and families we serve. They involve us with others and strengthen the identity of the profession. They give us the backing and professional voice we need to confront society and legislators about the injustices and realities of our situation and to initiate change. Participating in organizations helps us develop self-confidence and builds our self-esteem personally and professionally. There is enormous power in working together with a group of people in a political struggle. It increases one's sense of self in amazing and miraculous ways. And, dear early childhood educators, don't be deceived by politicians' rhetoric! We do have a political struggle on our hands in our profession. I want you to understand the enormity of society's statement to us when they do not require higher education and credentials for early childhood teachers. It keeps us ignorant and helpless. It victimizes and marginalizes us. Low compensation is only the half of it!

> Until all children in America have access to high-quality, developmentally appropriate early childhood and early grade experiences, and until all early childhood providers and teachers are able to receive the training and financial support they require to keep them in the field and ensure their commitment and competence, as many advocates as possible are needed to speak out on behalf of children. (Robinson and Stark 2002, 5)

How to Set Up a
Support-Supervision Group

The real issue for teachers, as for all of us, is not whether we do or do not possess prejudices, but whether we can honestly recognize them in ourselves. Only by admitting and facing our inevitable prejudices can we hope to deal with them effectively, to make up for them, compensate for them, or otherwise undo any damage caused by them. . . . To face this honestly is the first necessary step for moving on to more positive relationships between persons and groups.

Herbert M. Greenberg, *Teaching with Feeling*

In fact, teacher empowerment does not occur without reflection and the development of the means to express justifications. Without such empowerment, teachers may become victims of their personal biographies, systemic political demands, and ecological conditions, rather than making use of them in developing and sustaining worthwhile and significant change.

Virginia Richardson, "Significant and Worthwhile Change in Teaching Practice"

It's as if the two great movements of our time, those for social justice and for self-realization, were halves of a whole just waiting to come together into truly revolutionary groups.

Gloria Steinem, *Revolution from Within*

Developing communication skills (how to listen to others, how to tell "my" story) is a crucial component in anti-bias work. Listening to each other's stories helps us understand how people develop survival skills so that we are better able to negotiate our differences. If teachers are given the opportunity to reflect with others about some of these uncomfortable feelings, they might be able to change their practices or biased behaviors in more authentic ways. In addition, through discussion we learn about ourselves. In order to understand ourselves better, some of us need support or compassionate co-reflection with mentors, supervisors, colleagues, or support groups.

Reflective Practice

> Reflection has been recognized as a useful technique for helping teachers integrate the scientific and personal knowledge systems. It is assumed that as teachers reflect on their practices, they can make their understanding of classroom events more explicit, and therefore more amenable to control and direction. Teachers who reflect on how they feel and why they feel the way they do are in a better position to understand their interactions with others. (Bowman 1989)

NAEYC's National Institute for Early Childhood Professional Development has developed a conceptual framework that identifies key principles of an effective professional development system (NAEYC 1994). At each level, the professional is expected to engage in reflective practice that contributes to continuing professional development.

> Exemplary teachers participate in a wide range of reflective practices that reinforce their creativity, stimulate their personal growth, and enhance their professionalism. They exemplify the highest ethical ideals and embrace professional standards in assessing their practice. Ultimately, self-reflection contributes to teachers' depth of knowledge, skills, and dispositions and adds dignity to their practice. (NAEYC 1996, 94)

Reflective practice is not a new idea. John Dewey defines reflective thought as: "Active, persistent and careful consideration of any belief or supposed form of knowledge in the light of the grounds that support it and the further conclusions to which it tends" (Dewey 1933, 9). In *How We Think: A Restatement of the Relation of Reflective Thinking to the Educative Process*, Dewey talks about reflective thinking as having two phases where discomfort is considered part of the process as the thinker works with resolving doubt, perplexity, and mental difficulty. Teachers are encouraged to cultivate certain, specific attitudes toward reflective thinking such as open-mindedness, whole heartedness, and responsibility for facing the consequences. Dewey goes on to warn teachers about trying to please administrators or parents because very often these are the "chief forces that determine beliefs apart from and even contrary to the operations of intelligent thought" and "it may lead a person too readily to fall into the prejudices of others and may weaken his independence of judgment" (1933, 28–29).

There are different ways of looking at reflective practice. Much of the research looks at teachers' ability to assess a situation and make sense out of the experience. Each person makes a different sense or meaning. Supervisors or mentors assist some and some individuals do it alone. Self-reflection is a medium for self-awareness. For example, the idea of self-awareness is discussed as assisting teachers in their classroom practices and personal lives and is characterized as "valuable, perhaps indispensable" (Ayers 1989, ix). Ayers suggests that if teachers become more self-conscious, they could then become "more intentional, more able to endorse or reject aspects of their own teaching that they found hopeful or contrary, more able to author their own teaching scripts" (140).

In a later book, *To Teach: The Journey of a Teacher* (1993), Ayers uses his own autobiography and self-reflection, which he believes is crucial for teaching. He suggests that teachers should be asking: "Who are you? How did you come to take on your views and outlooks? What forces helped to shape you? What was it like for you to be ten? What have you made of yourself? Where are you heading?" and further states, "self-knowledge is most important (and least attended to)" (129).

One of the ways teacher educators and researchers discuss reflective practice is through the teachers telling their own stories (Ayers 1993, Clandinin, Davies, Hogan, and Kennard 1993, Goodson, 1992, Hall, Campbell, and Miech 1997). In this way, the researcher is able to understand how teachers develop values and beliefs and is able to assist them more effectively in understanding how those values affect decision making. In one case study, the teacher not only tells her story, but shares in the process of self-understanding. Implications of this study are that teachers need to be supported and considered as a part of their own process for change in future professional development (Yonemura 1986). These ideas further encourage teacher-educators in supporting or "growing" teachers in a collaborative way rather than top-down (Caruso and Fawcett 1986, Fenichel 1992, Jones 1993).

Virginia Richardson talks about teacher perceptions and beliefs about themselves as learners and teachers as she reviews the literature about making change in teachers' practice (Richardson 1990). Teachers have control over the decisions they make. Without their active involvement, autonomy, and reflection it seems difficult to make changes in classroom practice. Richardson mentions a number of case studies that demonstrate, for example, how a sixth-grade math teacher's beliefs about how children learn to read are strongly tied to his view of himself as a reader and how he learned to read. Richardson asks: "How then, are we to think about affecting change, other than through a type of individualistic, psychoanalytic approach to teacher education?" (13).

> Any of us who has had the good fortune . . . of befriending some-one who listens carefully to what we are saying and cares about what we are thinking, soon finds out that with regard to the most fundamental issues we are ambivalent, confused and find it difficult to know what we believe. (Brown 1982, 12)

Having outlined some of the problems of teacher education, Brown discusses the use of a new metaphor, namely therapy. Some of the features of therapy would not only "enable us to understand what we do in fact believe, but to help us find out what is behind those beliefs. What are the images, fears, joys, associations we hold onto that generate such beliefs?" (12).

Self-reflection is useful for teachers as they make moment-to-moment decisions in the classroom. It helps them understand why they do what they do, affects their perceptions and beliefs, and supports changes teachers make in curriculum and classroom management. Different ways of facilitating self-reflection are mentoring, in-service training or "growing teachers" through listening to their stories. Counseling therapy is suggested as a type of self-reflection that would affect change and enable educators to gain a deeper understanding of their attitudes or beliefs.

Support Groups for Teachers

Human, emotional qualities of the teacher are at the very heart of teaching (Greenberg 1969). According to Greenberg, no matter how much emphasis is placed on such other qualities in teaching as educational technique, technology, or equipment, the humanity of the teacher is the vital ingredient for children's learning. Teacher-educators should be concerned, in teacher preparation, about the study of the emotional life of the teacher.

"The behavior of a teacher, like that of everyone else, is a function of his concepts of self" (Combs 1965, 22). This concept of self will affect every aspect of a teacher's behavior and is, in turn, affected by attitudes, beliefs, and values. According to Combs, teacher-educators should be "deeply concerned" with the kinds of self-concepts teachers are developing in training. Teacher education needs to be more than instruction of subject matter, methodologies, or curriculum and even faculty should help teachers develop their inner selves.

In 1955, Jersild conducted a five-year study where he surveyed approximately one thousand people, some of whom had experienced psychotherapy and had been seeking to discover what the idea of self-understanding might mean in their work as teachers. The responses of the people indicated not only that the idea of self-understanding was an acceptable one, but also that many expressed a desire for help such as might be gotten from group therapy (Jersild 1955). The teachers involved in the study talked about feelings of loneliness and anxiety and suggested that they were serious in their search for intimate and personal meaning in what they were doing. Jersild recommended a form of group therapy under the leadership of a professional, specifically trained for such work, and stressed the importance of teachers facing themselves.

A teacher is more likely to become compassionate and understanding of the children through self-acceptance (Jersild 1954). "We must raise the question of personal significance in connection with everything we seek to learn and everything that is taught from the nursery school through postgraduate years" (Jersild 1955, 136). According to Jersild, the emotional life of a teacher is a dimension of teaching that is more often ignored than explored, and in the long run results in a loss to children. Unresolved emotional conflicts affect teachers' relationships with children, including attitudes toward their own self-worth, anger, hostility, sex, pride and shame, and acceptance and rejection. Teachers are unable to understand a child's anxiety and fears unless they are able to examine their own. Calling on teacher-educators to think about the implications for teacher preparation, Jersild has one broad principle to offer: "To gain in knowledge of self one must have the courage to seek it and the humility to accept what one might find" (1954, 412). This process might be painful or uncomfortable and might be sought out either in private therapy or in a group therapy situation.

Jersild further suggests that in a group setting teachers are able to learn to face themselves by the interactions and responses of the other participants toward them. "It is in a setting of joint and common work and airing of self with other people that some of the richest possibilities for self-examination can be found" (413). Jersild strongly urges the education community to add this type of support group to teacher preparation and ongoing staff development.

During the eighties, the organization of support or mutual assistance groups proliferated (Levine 1988). While reflecting the values of empowerment for people suffering from conditions attributed to oppressive social environments or those desiring to undertake personal change, the social support provided by these groups seemed to help their members in different ways. These types of groups were led by the group members themselves and not by a professional trained for such work, as Jersild suggested earlier. The group members no longer felt isolated. They shared feelings, which developed a sense of solidarity, and identified with one another in a way that enabled them to see that if one is able to change, so is the other.

"Spontaneously-developed" support groups for professional development are examined in what is considered to be the first study of its kind about teachers and support groups (Rich 1991). These groups have emerged in response to the needs of teachers. Most teachers work alone, behind closed classroom doors with little support while balancing personal and professional values with emotionally stressful classroom situations. The advantage of a professional support group according to Rich's study is that it provides personal support and a reference group "in which members are perceived as being like each other" (39).

One feminist researcher advocates developing groups for social change. "Revolutionary groups" should be "free, diverse, no bigger than the extended family—and everywhere" (Steinem 1993, 348). Basic guidelines for setting up "revolutionary groups" include describing the size of the group; recommending the duration, length of meeting for "meaningful change"; and that "no leader" and "confidentiality and honesty" would be prerequisites for all participants. Steinem suggests starting out with the question "What do you hope will change because of this group?" (357) and includes topics for discussion such as education, childhood, spirituality, and relationships.

> For all social justice movements and other efforts to make self-respecting change, these new-and-improved small groups could be a crucial bridge between organizations and the people they're designed to help; between personal experience and its political cause; between the present and the future. (Steinem 1993, 351)

Social change includes taking a stand against racism. Taking initiative against racism includes developing the skill of "support listening" which reinforces self-reflection while others listen to another talk about experiences, feelings, and plans (Vernon-Jones 1993). In order to develop this skill, it is suggested that teachers form support groups whereby they will use support listening and learn about racism in a safe environment. The difference between action groups, discussion groups, and support groups, according to Vernon-Jones, is that members of a support group build trust and thus will be able to "listen with caring attention to each member so each one can think through issues and work through feelings" (1993, 5).

Teachers are encouraged to find a support group and engage in consciousness-raising activities to enable themselves to understand their own biases better should they be interested in anti-bias work (Derman-Sparks 1989). By understanding the source of their own biases, teachers will then be able to help children with theirs. In a later report from the *Culturally Relevant Anti-Bias Leadership Project* (Cronin et al. 1998), Derman-Sparks encourages the reflective process through group work, and reminds us it is important to connect self-reflection with activism:

Doing culturally relevant anti-bias work requires growth at the personal level as well as in skills for creating professional and systemic change. Action without personal growth is an invitation to contribute to the problem one is trying to solve; however, personal growth without taking action in one's various communities becomes self-indulgence. (18)

During the late fifties and early sixties, teacher-educators suggested that "preparing teachers" should involve a development of awareness about their emotional life and that individual or group therapy would be a useful medium for self-understanding. In the eighties, support groups were referred to as *self-help groups* and were led by group members themselves. Derman-Sparks' groups supported a commitment to acting for change in the community.

Creating a Support-Supervision Group

In the quiet of my one-roomed schoolhouse in Israel, I dreamed of a support-supervision group for teachers. Once or twice I asked Zehava, my supervisor, why she did not organize such a group for us. I knew I was grappling with integrating my personal feelings with professional behaviors and interventions in the classroom. At staff development meetings I would often hear my colleagues talk in biased ways about children and families. I was sure we all needed supervision that would support our feelings, and, at the same time help us make connections between the personal and professional. Zehava concluded that such a group sounded too much like therapy and would not be suitable for everyone.

My dream was realized in the spring of 1995 when my dissertation committee allowed me to facilitate an anti-bias support-supervision group for early childhood teachers and administrators in Buffalo, New York (Meyer 1997). At first the members of the committee were concerned about the rationale for such a group. They voiced similar concerns as Zehava had done in Israel. It sounded too much like therapy. While one person of the committee applauded the idea of some kind of therapy support for teachers, the others wanted me to make sure it would not become that. I was given permission to facilitate the group and conduct a study at the same time.

I did not want the purpose of the group to be mutual assistance or self-indulgence. Instead, the group would give support and supervision. Participants were encouraged to make connections between their emotions and biases specifically with interactions and behaviors with children and families. Therefore, I named the group *support-supervision*. At the final session, group members were asked to choose pseudonyms in order to ensure their confidentiality as they had agreed to be quoted in the written section of the research project. (All names of the participants used in this chapter are pseudonyms.) They tell the story in their own words through written journals, and the interviews shared with Yi Hao, a graduate student.

> . . . it was amazing that the group for these two hours every Tuesday were able to really search into themselves about different issues . . . this group serves more from inside out.
>
> —Gloria

> It's a place to talk about the private stuff of your life or of your work. And it always does seem to tie back into your private life. If you started at private life it ties back into work. If you start at work, it ties back into private life. They're just interconnected . . . it just evolves, and that's what excites.
>
> —Hattie

> . . . we discuss things. People's biases and how our own bias can be portrayed onto the children . . . we talked about personal things amongst the group members . . . Just talking about how our biases affect ourselves and how it affects the children we deal with every day. And then how, if they come from different backgrounds . . . how that would affect us in dealing with them.
>
> —Chloe

Teachers and directors from four childcare centers voluntarily participated in the support group. They met with me, their facilitator, for a period of twenty weeks at ten bi-weekly sessions each lasting two hours. At first with the help of a childcare organization, I sent letters randomly to thirty-five childcare centers. I invited teachers to join a support group if they were interested in implementing the anti-bias curriculum. Originally, fourteen women joined; three were administrators, and eleven were teachers who worked with children ages six weeks to five years. Four teachers left the group during the first six weeks. One described feeling discomfort with the level of intimacy and personal nature of discussion.

> You know, if someone was upset, she'd (the facilitator) make sure that we all recognized that and if someone responded in a certain kind of way she would ask them about it or ask them to clarify it, why they responded in that way or whatever. To some extent it makes people uncomfortable but I think that was part of the learning experience. Because it's all about communication and communication makes people feel uncomfortable depending on what's being said.
>
> —Danielle

Participation in the group included:

- Attending ten bi-weekly support group sessions,

- Writing a personal journal,

- Reading Derman-Sparks' *Anti-Bias Curriculum: Tools for Empowering Young Children* (at the beginning of the group sessions, participants received a copy of the book which they were allowed to keep if they remained in the group until the end of the twenty-week period),

- Allowing the group sessions to be audiotaped,

- Agreeing to be observed by Nancy (a colleague and graduate student) for two of the sessions,

- Participating in an in-depth interview for an hour and a half with Yi, and

- Answering questionnaires about their expectations for the support-supervision group experience, at the beginning and end of the twenty-week period.

Within the sessions, participants were encouraged to discuss personal feelings and, at times, they were given specific exercises or assignments.

For example, they were asked to draw and describe a picture of their family, and, during Women's History Month, asked to define what it meant for them to be a woman. Hattie's poem, written in a group exercise, follows.

> **To Be a Woman**
>   Wo
>   man -
>   Whoa - man -
>   Slow down man -
>   How much can you do in one day mohn!!
>   mom.
>   Eons, years of *her*story
>   So much hidden
>   mystery
>   of life
>   and bonds
>   of lives
>   beyond
>   our own
>   Interwoven webs

Support group sessions were held on-site at one of the childcare centers in the evening. The meeting place constituted a large conference room with a number of comfortable chairs and a long table. It was the same throughout the twenty-week period of group sessions and was conducive to a relaxed atmosphere.

My experience was accompanied by a personal journal and I audiotaped and transcribed all support-supervision group sessions. Prior to each support group session, I received an hour of supervision from a professional counselor. I shared my feelings and biases with him about what had happened with the participants two weeks before. Through discussion with him, I made changes, modifications, or chose interventions that seemed appropriate to the emotional issues that came up within the group. In addition, his guidance helped me understand the dynamics of interactions among group members and between them and myself.

I brought to the group my own subjectivity and bias, knowledge of early childhood education, and some counseling skills. As I worked to understand the data collected and to facilitate the group, I tried to make sense about which part belonged to me, and which the members. I realized that many times I challenged the participants to search for connections between personal biases and interactions with children or teachers in their programs. At times I felt I succeeded. It was difficult at first when I did not. I learned, time and time again, that my biases and feelings affected how I heard the participants. By becoming intimately involved with the way these women were feeling about their personal and professional lives, and often sharing my personal background, I was able, many times, to challenge them and myself. For a period of four months, it seemed as if perceptions about themselves and society were broadened, and awareness about bias and our work became, as Chloe described it, "big."

> Bias would be a whole bunch of stuff. . . . Yeah, it could be the way a family is. It's not the mother/father anymore. It could be sexual orientation. It could be culture . . . like a person with a physical handicap who's in a wheelchair. You know it's just the way you speak about someone I guess . . . or even body language towards someone . . . facial expressions, tone of voice, you know talking down to someone. . . . I don't even know if I could define it because it's so wide. I don't know if I could give a pat answer for it. . . . Because it's all around us all the time. I have written in my journal that it's subtle, you know . . . it's a big answer.
>
> —Chloe, interview

What Did We Learn?

Derman-Sparks (1989) identifies four goals for self-education and states that a support group is essential for preparing and implementing an anti-bias curriculum.

> Increase awareness of your attitudes about gender, race, ethnicity, and different physical abilities; learn to identify ways that institutional racism, sexism and handicappism affect your program; gain an understanding of how young children develop identity and attitudes; plan ways to introduce anti-bias curriculum into your setting. (111)

All ten of the women in the group talked about the experience as beneficial to them. Six expressed ideas for future plans including starting similar groups in other centers, experimenting with the duration of the group, involving more than one center, and using this model for pre-service teacher education.

> I think it's really important and I don't know how you would get more women to do this. I'm saying women because that's mostly who is in daycare . . . and I would like to know how you would take it a step further and encourage other women who aren't really pro-diversity to begin with, to come and take a chance. . . . See, in the group I think what happened was people were able to explore stuff, listen to things and grow from it . . . and I wish there was a way that those women could try out talking how they feel. 'Cause then they would hear that it is really hard for me too. It's not easy. But I think that they think that's just the way I am and that it is easy to make those decisions.
>
> —Hattie, interview

> The group itself needs to go longer. Because we were just coming into our own, so to speak. Really starting to do the hard work. The first four to five sessions easily went a lot too, not that we didn't deal with things, but we dealt with them at a different level. The best impact is coming now and I hate to see us quit. So, going into it I think it's more of an ongoing process . . . if it were an ongoing outlet for a professional, I would leave it as that . . . I think that this type of group should be a part certainly of studies to prepare to be a teacher . . . we have to understand a little bit about what happens in here. You know, we're giving to children who are so vulnerable. Who need such a safety net. Who need, need to feel that safety. Pardon the redundancy.
>
> —Simcha

Teachers often experience loneliness in their work as they spend long hours with young children, having to make moment-by-moment decisions. Many of these decisions are confused or obstructed by bias. All ten women described feeling a fundamental change in their perceptions about bias. They made connections between those perceptions and their interactions with children or staff. For example, in the final session, Hattie disclosed to the group that a child, with whom she had been struggling for many months, was clearly disappointed when he heard she would be leaving his class for a new position in her center. She described that her discomfort at his anger had decreased because, with the group's help, she was able to connect her own feelings of anger, which had reminded her of a difficult relationship in her past. She had identified the boy in her class as having similar characteristics with the man of that relationship.

> Remember the struggle I had about that thing with the angry stuff I had with him? By working through it here, some of it, I was able to then work with him in a different way . . . and I was saying that when he found out that I wasn't gonna be the teacher in the room anymore, he was jumping up and down, literally jumping up and down going: "No, you can't go! No you can't go!" I looked at him and said, "T. H. is that you?" I couldn't believe it. Obviously we'd gotten somewhere because he would never have done that, I don't think.
>
> —Hattie, final group session

In a support group situation, teachers were able to explore emotional, personal issues of bias, and identify with others in similar situations. Although the process was at times uncomfortable, it appears that sharing the experience with others, in a trusting and respectful environment, helped some of them undertake personal change. Two specific issues, dealt with intensively by the group, were beneficial to the women in their personal and professional lives and are worthy of attention.

Sexual Orientation

> I told the people who missed the last meeting that I was a lesbian. That discussion led into one about Gloria's students. It was a quite thorough discussion around issues of gender and sexuality (in a broad sense). This discussion seemed to be exactly what this group is about. We talked about our personal feelings about it but also talked about the practical (which is what I like to do!) solutions about talking to parents, helping individual children as well as groups of children deal with differences— helping the individual accept and be themself and teach others to treat each other with respect.
>
> —Katherine, journal

Participants were able to discuss the issue of sexual orientation in a trusting and respectful environment. Two of the women came out. Both of them, as well as those who received this information, needed support in processing their emotions. Teachers and administrators benefited from the experience of trusting each other enough to share these intimate feelings. Those who received support by the group as they disclosed their lifestyle described feeling stronger and more confident in dealing with life on both personal and professional levels.

> The discussion of "touchy feely" was great. It touched on the heart of the gender issues. I can appreciate Katherine's sensitivity about how she might be misinterpreted by staff. As a lesbian I think about these perceptions and probably lend much more importance to how actions might be read than necessary.
>
> —Simcha, journal

> Simcha surprised me the most. I feel she had a tremendous amount of courage to tell everyone, many of them strangers, that she is gay. I didn't know that about her . . . she reminds me of my sister . . . who is also gay. My sister and I are identical twins— isn't it interesting that we have the same genetic makeup and were raised in the same environment yet she is gay and I am not?
>
> —Danielle, journal

> Sexual orientation—never been exposed as much as this group— I feel very comfortable with this, never thought I would.
>
> —Chloe, journal

I started to think about how early childhood programs support gay families in general. If they are not dealing with it, which seems to be the case according to experiences from group members, how are teachers, families, and consequently, children, coping with the realities of their lives? The question of sexual orientation is an emotional subject, connected to feelings of fear and guilt, and concepts of morality and religious ideologies. The support-supervision group proved to be an effective environment. Participants were able to process a range of complex emotions and values, develop understanding of homophobia, and increase acceptance of themselves and others.

Anger

A number of group sessions dealt with anger. All of the women in the group experienced discomfort about expressing anger. Two women described concerns about angry children in their classrooms. Some advice was shared between group members. For example, introducing a punching cushion or areas of quiet and privacy for children who were overstimulated. Teachers were able to resolve difficult situations with angry children successfully partly because of the advice shared, but, more specifically, they realized that some of their anger had been transferred onto children from their own personal situations. Soon after one of the women had processed her own anger and fear about her mother's illness, she expressed that the children in her class did not seem as angry to her as before. Hattie described an improvement in her relationship with a little boy in her class, T. H. This had been anger about a past love that she felt she processed with the group.

Group members were able to explore some of these intense and frightening emotions. Most of the women described feeling generally more comfortable with their emotions. As a result they were more accepting of children's emotions. Ultimately, this directly affected a change in behaviors toward children in their classrooms. Directors described that they were more aware and accepting of emotions of teachers they were supervising in their centers.

Awareness of Bias

All group members described a sense of heightened awareness about bias as it related to themselves personally, children in classrooms, or with teachers in their centers. All of them made connections between how their own prejudices affected how they treat children, families, colleagues, or, even, board members. Evidence of this was supported by data from all participants, including definitions of bias, transcripts of the support group process, journals, and interviews. For about half of the women, it was surprising for them to discover in fact, just how biased they were.

Some described awareness as heightened *consciousness*. Two teachers expressed that some of their interactions with and perceptions of angry children in their classrooms had been directly because of unconscious emotional issues. This is an important point to consider: Bias or unconscious emotions influence teachers' interactions or perceptions. Many times, the results are harmful to children and families. Taken a step further, they are harmful to groups of people.

Heightened awareness or consciousness is an important step in the process of self-reflection and, consequently, the ability to make changes. However, it requires taking risks and, for many, that feels uncomfortable or unsafe when experienced alone. One teacher-educator suggests being a "resistance fighter on behalf of children" (Ayers 1993, 131). That is a tough order for teachers unless they are given support and a safe environment in which to explore those risks of *self-criticism* that he recommends.

Counseling

Facilitating a person's journey from unconscious to conscious leads us into the language of counseling. Some of the participants raised this question in different ways. They reflected on this aspect of the support group in journals and interviews. For example, when asked what was the worst thing she had experienced in the support group sessions, Lydia talked about intensity:

> The conversation in the session would get so intense you would have trouble sleeping that evening. That would be the worst thing, because it was uncomfortable the next day.
>
> —Lydia

Katherine suggested that people had left the group in the beginning because of the discomfort at opening up. The women talked about this at the final session.

> Well, we started off with probably twice as much staff as we ended up with. And I think a lot of people are very uncomfortable being so open and personal.
>
> —Katherine

I feel at times the group has gone off the track in the sense that
we have turned it into a therapy session—which has worked out
well for some but others have been put off by it.

—Chloe, journal

Simcha described the group as being different to regular staff meetings. She attributed that to the emotional nature of the group.

[N]ot that it was unprofessional, but we crossed a line that would
not necessarily happen in a staff meeting. The emotions . . .
people were very free to speak, very free to support or criticize,
which happened over time as well as we became more comfortable with each other. Um, it was much more emotionally based.
. . . You typically would not have, or hopefully would not have,
staff members crying in a staff meeting. And it was not unusual
for someone to become emotional to the point of tears in our
group.

—Simcha

Simcha raised an important consideration when she used the expression, *crossed a line*. Questions are raised by crossing that line:
Should teacher education and counseling become integrated or linked
together in some way? Should self-reflection relate only to cognitive
and social awareness? Do educators have a right to emotional self-
awareness? Or, as Katherine asked in the reunion session two years
after the support group, "Is it even a responsibility?"

Self-reflection does not relate only to cognitive and social awareness. Counselors, for example, explore and understand their own personal bias, attitudes, and emotions so that they will interact with
clients more effectively. In some situations, counselors are required
to have supervision for that very reason. In fact, they are encouraged
to develop personal, emotional awareness. There is no support for
teachers to explore or understand their own emotions. It is definitely
not required and sometimes not even mentioned. And yet, teachers
continue to deal with many uncomfortable, emotional issues all day.

In the end, counseling was not considered a limitation of the support group or of the study. Although therapy-type issues arose, the
group attempted no therapy per se. It did, however, raise important

concerns for creating a safe environment for participants in future groups of this nature.

> Opening up one's private life to others is making oneself vulnerable. Some may be uncomfortable with this if they feel it is something expected of them or imposed upon them. . . . Participation in this kind of support group should be voluntary. It should be made clear from the beginning that there will be sessions that are intimate and personally revealing. Some counseling/therapy is involved for participating members. . . . The facilitator should be properly trained in counseling and education when working with personal issues and biases in a support group for teachers.
>
> —Nancy, participant observer

The Facilitator's Role

According to the group, the role of the support-supervision group facilitator should include four points. The facilitator

1. should not be an immediate supervisor to any one member of the support group
2. should have counseling skills
3. should receive counseling supervision to ensure a safe, trusting, and respectful environment
4. should have a clearly defined role.

The facilitator would have to deal with different emotional situations within the group. For example, one member of the group became anxious when other people were sad or angry. She tried to placate and would often intercede and prevent other women from processing their feelings. The facilitator would have to deal with group dynamics like these in a way that would provide a trusting and respectful environment for everyone.

> Childcare workers, as other people, often have intense personal struggles to contend with. Many people are afraid to address emotions because they can be so powerful . . . the facilitator should be trained in counseling and education when working with personal issues and biases in a support group of teachers.

. . . Once such intimate emotions are shared with supervisors, it may be difficult to separate work and professional life from private and personal life . . . the facilitator should be a person other than the immediate supervisor of any of the members of the support group.

—Nancy, participant observer

It is important for the facilitator of such a group to develop a trusting and respectful environment. Counseling skills such as active listening, and the ability to explore and confront difficult feelings with the participants are necessary. All the women described the importance of feeling safe when talking about feelings such as anger, fear, shame, or guilt. Self-reflection was uncomfortable for some. Gloria and Danielle talked about discomfort as a way to "rattle" or "shake people up" into making changes. Simcha called it "risky." Danielle described communication as sometimes being painful.

In order to ensure the safety of group members, I sought out supervision from an experienced and professional counselor. At each session with him, I examined my own emotions that were aroused in support group sessions. At times, I worked on understanding how others might be feeling. At others, I explored my own feelings. In the beginning it was difficult for me to let go of a cognitive level of discussion and I seemed to prevent emotional situations from becoming too intense. I experienced fear of confronting (in a counseling sense) or of what Katherine had termed, "getting past what you're thinking into what you're feeling."

I named one of my supervision sessions in my journal, "help me with M." Together with the counselor, I explored my discomfort with a member of the group who continuously interrupted others in an aggressive manner, usually when they needed to talk about difficult emotions. Talking about it with the counselor helped me understand that, in fact, M was becoming anxious with the emotional situation in the group and needed help, herself, at those moments.

In the beginning, I noticed that I laughed at moments when situations became serious or intimate. I named that session in my journal, "How do I take myself seriously?" I worked with the supervisor on my fears of expressing and accepting others' emotions. It became important to me to ensure a safe environment for the group and myself. As I assisted group members in identifying how bias might be obstructing or influencing their interactions with children, it made sense for me to go through a similar process with the counseling supervisor. A clear example of this was when it came time for the support group sessions to end.

Confronting my own subjectivity was essential in the process of separation and clarification of boundaries. This was a point at which I became joined with the women in the group. Separation was difficult for me. This resulted in some confusion and anxiety in one or two of the final sessions. I had become caring of the group members and was concerned about leaving them. Personally, I was experiencing anxiety of separation for two reasons. I felt the strength and support of this group of women for myself, and wanted to take care of them forever. Their personal and professional lives had become important to me. Struggling through these difficult emotions and processing them with my supervisor enabled me to clarify my goals. Finally I was able to help the group members understand and accept that the group sessions, as we knew them, would end.

It was necessary for me to help the group focus on topics, whether they were curriculum-related or emotional issues. Hattie described it, "not allowing us to skirt an issue." Nancy noted: "Group discussions which include personal issues can easily veer off track. A trained and professional facilitator is necessary to tie the personal issues back into professional ones." Nine of the ten women thought it was important for me not to be personally involved so that I was able to include everyone and make it safe. I often discussed this with my supervisor. We explored the idea that the group might become a self-help model and my role might change to one of participant. I was feeling pulled by dynamics within the group to become one of them. After many discussions he helped me clarify the boundaries. This became beneficial for support group members as well. "Feeling safe to feel pain together" (my journal).

Childcare, a Women's Issue

We all wrote journals during the four-month period of support group sessions. I explained, at the first meeting, that journal writing was voluntary. The purpose of the journals was a way for the women to express themselves privately if there were issues they were uncomfortable sharing within the larger group. Eight of the ten participants kept journals. Two did not write at all. One wrote regularly, describing it as "valuable for reflection," and enjoyable. All eight journals were well-written in terms of the women expressing how they felt about group sessions, personal issues, and recommendations for the future. Nine of them talked about not being good at writing. A couple of them spoke of themselves as "bad at writing things down" or "doing a bad job of writing." Hattie and Katherine did not think they wrote well either when, in fact, their journals were prolific and well-written:

> I don't like writing a lot. And [pause] some of it is I don't think I'm good with words in terms of saying, putting my feelings into words.
>
> —Katherine

> For anyone else it would be pretty bad reading. It's not the best reading but for myself I am able to work some stuff out there.
>
> —Hattie

Although the evidence was not conclusive or overwhelming in any way, the women's doubts about their ability to write raised some questions for me about early childhood teachers in general. My own bias influenced my interpretation and curiosity as to why 90 percent of the group described themselves as bad writers. Once again I joined with the group members. As a teacher, I have moved in and out of confidence many times throughout my life about my own intellectual ability, and I wondered if this was one of the reasons for these women's perceptions of themselves as writers. I remembered how I chose to become a teacher when I was young. Or did I? In fact, when I was young, I do not remember thinking about it very much at all. At some point in my youth I had dreamed of becoming a journalist, musician, or perhaps an actress.

Women are socialized from a young age to believe that there are few career options for them, and that they should choose nurturing professions such as childcare, teaching, or nursing. When asked why they chose childcare as a profession, all ten women gave similar reasons: "I wanted to since I was a child," "I love kids," "I kind of fell into it," and one actually said, "Teaching is something I've always wanted to do . . . I've never really thought of anything else to do."

As discussed in Chapter 4, childcare is not high up in the educational hierarchy, among other issues of compensation, education, and professionalism. Even many early childhood teachers themselves do not have high regard for childcare providers. The support-supervision group became beneficial for the women's self-esteem. Some of them described feeling stronger, more confident and able to make changes. For example, Hattie was able to change curriculum decisions in her classroom even though her colleagues at the center disapproved. She called herself an activist. Katherine and Simcha disclosed their sexual orientation and both described feeling stronger and more assertive because of the support of the group. Simcha moved in together with her companion and came out publicly. Danielle created a "Social Awareness Group" in her center. Half of the participants became involved in the local childcare organization either at staff networking or advocacy levels. Hattie made conscious changes regarding herself and the angry children in her classroom. Gloria chose her pseudonym from "Gloria Steinem" expressing a newfound feeling of confidence through her new name.

How Could the Support-Supervision Group Have Been Done Better?

African American, Native American, Hispanic, or Asian cultures were not represented in the group. Neither were men. Although an invitation letter was sent to over thirty childcare centers throughout the Western New York region, participants who volunteered were all Caucasian women. In all the childcare centers that were informed about the group, there are less than 5 percent male teachers. This might have explained why there were no male participants. Reasons why people of color did not volunteer are unclear. This was a limitation. The group dealt with issues of age, gender, religion, and sexual orientation. However, culture was dealt with theoretically and not on as emotional a level as sexual orientation, for example. There were some discussions about celebrating cultural holidays.

I just finished calling the group to confirm plans for our Seder. I don't know if I can effectively comment on how excited I am about all of this, but of course I'll give it a stab. Everyone sounds genuinely interested in participating. Some, like Molly, are really looking forward to coming. Even as an adult, I am finding myself to be so pleased that others are interested and curious about my Judaism. Can you imagine how children must feel? This has great implications for our work. Children, like adults, need to feel that we are genuinely interested in the specific aspects of their lives that they feel are important.

—Simcha, journal

Oh, I actually went to a social event. Meaning, some of us from the group got together and had a Seder, which is a Jewish holiday. So, I did that with them. That was nice. Cause I have no social life [laughs].

—Hattie

When relating to gender bias, participants expressed it as women's issues and needs. Some of the participants named the group: "Women's Group." Male gender issues were mentioned in passing and dealt with theoretically. While members of the group felt comfortable to talk to each other, this was a limitation. Different cultures and both genders should be represented when organizing a support-supervision group.

A support group such as this should have a definite beginning and end. It should not go on for an endless time. Everybody's issues need not be resolved.

—Nancy, participant observer

Length of time seemed to be a limitation for the group members. Nine of the women wanted the group to continue and some felt there were issues left unresolved. Length of the support-supervision group was defined by the research study. However, similar groups might continue for a longer period of time, depending on the needs of its members. Although length of time was clearly defined at the beginning of the group, participants expressed disappointment and anger about its conclusion, and negotiated intensely for its continuation towards the

end. Simcha reiterated her feelings about this limitation two years
after the group had ended.

> Getting started obviously required our group to get to know each
> other on an intimate basis. It seems to me that the issues sur-
> rounding bias are so deeply rooted in our personalities that we
> must first establish a groundwork that can be easily integrated
> into consideration of the professional issues. Without that level
> of comfort, it is difficult to truly explore the impact of bias in
> our work . . . I think that the trust issue is big. . . .
>
> —Simcha, written comments after the reunion session

With regard to this study, the length of the group limited the data
itself. Had the group been a few months longer, different issues might
have been presented or evidence stronger on certain themes. For example, I would have loved to explore further "childcare, a women's
issue."

A Support-Supervision Group Is Beneficial
for Self-Reflection

While I, as researcher and facilitator, observed and challenged the
women to expand perceptions of bias with relation to their interactions with children, I was challenged at the same time. Emotional
awareness of bias was shared and articulated by group members and
myself, in the support group and in the written account. All therefore,
shared benefits.

> Oh yeah, I mean I want to add it to my resume . . . what we said
> mattered . . . if we could condense it I would love staff to read
> it . . . assistant teachers, directors.
>
> —Chloe, reunion session

> There's a real ownership for all of us because of the participa-
> tion . . . a pride in that.
>
> —Katherine, reunion session

The *Anti-Bias Support-Supervision Group* was beneficial for teachers
and administrators in a number of ways: support for self-reflection,

heightened awareness of bias and prejudice, understanding connections between the personal and professional, strengthening of self-understanding and confidence, and positive changes in behaviors toward children. Teachers treat children as they are treated (Katz 1993). In that case, if we want teachers to treat children fairly, to listen to, to accept, and to enhance their self-identity, supervisors and educators must do the same for teachers. Some form of support for in-depth, compassionate co-reflection about bias and emotional awareness is necessary for fundamental change in attitudes and acceptance of diversity.

In-depth self-reflection is uncomfortable at times. People dropped out of the support-supervision group for that reason. Espinosa identifies self-reflection as an important quality, which separates great leaders from opportunistic leaders (1997). Self-reflection is not always an easy or comfortable experience. According to Espinosa, it is a struggle at times and a

> willingness to engage in the daily struggle of confronting one's limitations and investing in character development . . . those who become respected leaders over time embody these personal qualities that are born of struggle, self-knowledge, and personal development. (Espinosa 1997, 98–99)

In her interview, Simcha suggested that early childhood student teachers would benefit from a support group that would challenge their perceptions of bias. There are, in fact, some programs that integrate emotional awareness into the curriculum for undergraduate and graduate student teachers in early education. From conversations with teacher-educators about programs at Bank Street, Pacific Oaks, Wheelock College, and the Erikson Institute, it was clear that self-reflection and emotional awareness is an integral part of the curriculum for developing teachers (Garbarino 1997, Derman-Sparks 1992, Ayers 1992).

Resolving issues of bias is a process, and teachers benefit from ongoing support for self-reflection. Length of time is worthy of further thought: Would they need support-supervision indefinitely or for specific periods of time? Six months or a year might be enough for teachers to develop skills needed to change old attitudes and perceptions. In pre- or in-service teacher education, cost effectiveness is often an issue. However, how high is the price when we neglect this area of staff development?

At a lecture about multiple intelligence theory, Howard Gardner said that schools do not have to be the way we remember them (1993). We need to consider how we are helping teachers understand their own emotions so that they will be able to create environments different from what they remember. My study certainly did not solve the problems of bias, nor give all the answers about self-reflection and awareness. However, it did broaden perspectives and supported teachers in making some changes in their personal and professional lives. All the women were encouraged to think about ways in which to implement an anti-bias curriculum, and some actively introduced discussion and materials in their classrooms and centers. Some felt strengthened enough to think in terms of becoming activists.

> Actually, I think one of the most helpful things was it helped me build trust in other people. Because we talked about some very personal and painful things. And we were able to be honest with each other and sometimes disagree and there was even anger expressed. But at the end, everyone still respected and treated each other with respect . . . I think it is helpful in anti-bias. It is not directly related but I think getting through any bias the trust issue is what's important.
>
> —Katherine

Courage and Compassion

When teachers face themselves, they face a hard struggle;
but they may also look forward to great rewards. The
greatest of these rewards is growth in compassion.
Compassion is inextricably linked to acceptance of self
and of others. It is the ultimate expression of emotional
maturity. . . . Compassion is stronger than anger,
mightier than love, more powerful than fear. It gives the
measure of a person's strength as a human being. It is
not the emotion of the weak. It is the hard-gotten
property of the strong.

Arthur Jersild, *When Teachers Face Themselves*

When I was nine-years-old I remember my mother running out into the night because she had heard a child crying in a car that was parked near our house. I awoke to her throwing on her robe and running out saying something like, "That's enough, I can't take it anymore. I am going to see what's happening out there!" I sat and waited by the window for her return. I was anxious. I could hear the child's screams and the night was dark outside. It all felt quite ominous, especially my mother's fear for that child. She had spent some minutes out by the car talking to the parents. The child's crying had subsided. She came back into the house and mumbled something about the parents being drunk and therefore shouting at their child. She shook her head in sorrow at how the child was treated. I remember looking at my mother and feeling pride in her. If I had been old enough, I might have given her a hug right then and there and told her how proud I was of her. Instead, as a child I watched and listened quietly and went back to bed.

Children learn from what the significant adults in their lives do and say. So often, as adults, we forget that children are watching what we do and listening to what we say. Physically, they are below our eye level and sometimes we forget they are there. Most of what we teach young children about our values is indirect, through behaviors and not, as many would think, through formal instruction. I have a bumper sticker on my car that says "It is never okay to hit a child." I like it because if a child reads that or is told what it says, she will know that someone out there will make a stand for her. She is not alone.

She was always doing things like that, my mother. Having suffered her share of abuse as a child she was sensitive to all children everywhere. It could be like the incident of the crying child, or once when she told one of her close friends in a stern and direct manner that her child would die if she did not seek a physician's help immediately. She did, indeed, save that child's life as a result of her insistence. I felt pride in the way she would fearlessly march into situations to save a child.

The Nature of Compassion

Over the years I have purchased a number of posters from an organization called *Syracuse Cultural Workers*. Each day early in the morning when I enter my office, I spend a few minutes quietly reading the captions on the posters. I like to surround myself with inspirational messages that help reinforce my beliefs and give me the emotional stamina to continue the work that I do. There is a poster with an almost life-sized picture of the African American, lesbian poet, Audre Lorde, her arms stretched out widely as if to embrace the viewer. The caption reads: "When I dare to be powerful, to use my strength in the service of my vision, then it becomes less and less important whether I am afraid." Another poster, which hangs directly over my desk, has a large photograph of a number of diverse infants lying in a circle in the middle of the page. Underneath the picture of the children the caption reads:

> Hello, babies. Welcome to Earth.
> It's hot in the summer and cold in the winter.
> It's round and wet and crowded.
> At the outset, babies, you've got about a hundred years here.

There's only one rule that I know of, babies:
God damn it, you've got to be kind.

Kurt Vonnegut, Jr.
[italics mine]

The last line of that caption sums up much of what, in my opinion, is of paramount importance as we do the work we do, and specifically as it relates to an anti-bias approach. The term *kind* seems simple in this caption, but still somehow it manages to conjure up for us the stern, almost of-dire-importance way it relays the message to us. I do not think of kindness as *in being nice to someone* (whatever that means!). I think of it in the deeper, more complex sense of *compassion*.

Compassion is an intellectual and emotional understanding of the human condition. Some say that it comes to those who have suffered and allowed themselves to develop empathy.

To develop real empathy, we must at one time or another have permitted ourselves to feel frightened, overwhelmed or helpless. Indeed, a certain amount of strength is required for us to open ourselves up and express vulnerability. (Person 2002, 26)

When you feel empathy or compassion, you are able to understand what someone else might be going through without judgment. You do not pity the person but understand what they might be feeling. You come to know what it is like to walk in their shoes. *Compassion* is such a difficult word to define because it is a combination of feeling and understanding. How do we authentically define it? The source of *compassion* is from Latin, *com* and *pati*, which mean to *bear* or *suffer*. The Merriam-Webster dictionary defines compassion as: "Sympathetic consciousness of others' distress together with a desire to alleviate it."

When we take on the challenge of an anti-bias approach we become activists. I remember once seeing these words of Martin Luther King, Jr., written on a postcard: "The silence of good people is worse than bigoted acts." Once we become aware of how prejudice causes discrimination and inequity how could we be silent in the face of bigoted acts? I found this definition of *compassion* at www.visualthesaurus.com/index.jsp: "A deep awareness of and sympathy for another's suffering—the humane quality of understanding the suffering of others and wanting to do something about it." When we develop compassion, we will be more likely to speak out if we witness an individual or groups of people being treated unfairly.

At our center we help young children to say assertively: "I don't like it when you do or say that." We extend that expression to create an activist group by saying "*We* don't like it when you do or say that." A few years ago one of our four-year-olds told his grandfather to stop tickling him by saying: "Grandfather, I don't like it when you do that!" Tickling is not always an enjoyable experience for young children. Many children feel helpless and afraid when adults hold them down to tickle them. They are unable to tell the very people they are trying to please that they are afraid. The mother of the child at our Center was delighted and grateful that her child was able to tell his grandfather to stop tickling him. She thanked me for teaching him to make a stand for himself in that way.

Recently one of our teachers read to our preschoolers, *Contemplating Your Belly Button* by Jun Nanao. On the last page of the book is a photograph of many pink-colored belly buttons. One of the children called out, "Where is N's belly button?" She was referring to an African American child in the class. The teacher took out a pad and pencil and together with the children they composed a letter to the publisher. They wrote:

> To whom it may concern: Recently our Preschool class read *Contemplating Your Belly Button* by Jun Nanao as part of our study of the body. We really enjoyed the book. At the end of the book, there are several photographs of belly buttons. One of the children in the class was concerned that there were no photos of "brown" (African American) belly buttons and was wondering why. I thought that maybe it was because the book was originally published in Japan and maybe there are not a lot of African American people or belly buttons in Japan. If you know the answer to our question, our class would appreciate if you replied to our letter at the address below.

The teacher and the concerned child signed the letter together. Less than a month later the publisher replied that they were pleased to hear from the readers telling them of their worries about their friend. In fact the belly buttons depicted were those of Japanese children. "Looks can be deceiving since their skin tone is similar to those of other nationalities," the publisher explained. They suggested that our teacher send a picture of our African American child's belly button to display on the publisher's website along with our concerns and suggestions. We did—after we had received permission from her parents. The children learned that not only could they speak out when they felt a classmate had been excluded, but something could be done about it.

In *The Contract of Mutual Indifference* (1999), author and scholar Norman Geras gives a detailed description of the atrocities of the Holocaust and, specifically, he writes about how people stood by, turned away, and did nothing. He asks us to "face up to things unpleasant," because since the Holocaust there have been many occasions where humankind continues to stand by and do nothing to prevent genocide and mass hunger the world over. His discussion tries to understand why there seems to be a universal lack of compassion.

On the other hand, Geras describes many testimonies about non-Jewish people, who went out of their way often putting themselves at risk or endangering their own families in order to help Jews escape or by hiding them from the Nazis. He reminds us that "the human record is replete also with acts of moral heroism and moral excellence, and with ordinary, unspectacular day-to-day decency" and that "mutual human sympathy and beneficence run both deep and wide" (1999, 119). Therefore, Geras does not allow us to conclude that all is lost or that all of humankind is without compassion. Indeed, he warns us that we have a moral option and obligation not to give up hope even when we have witnessed the worst side of our nature as human beings.

> To accept the world as it (more or less) is, is to help prolong a state of grave danger. This world accommodating and countenancing too much of what ought not to be tolerated—plain, persistent injustice, stark, avoidable human suffering—is a world very receptive to present and future atrocity, a world overpopulated with bystanders. It is one in which the idea is harder and harder to resist that just anything at all may be done to people while others look on; and there be no consequence. As long as the situation lasts, it degrades the moral culture of the planet. It poisons the conscience of humankind. (Geras 1999, 121)

Rebecca Walker is the daughter of the African American author Alice Walker and white, Jewish lawyer Mel Leventhal. As an author herself, she writes about her struggles and the challenges she faced growing up in a mixed-race family. In *Black White and Jewish: Autobiography of a Shifting Self* (2001), Rebecca Walker describes the development of her own identity and realizes that she must include others even as she feels identified with one or other of what she terms *my people*. She says that compassion is when we identify with and have an "affinity with [all] beings who suffer" (306).

> Do I identify with the legacy of slavery and discrimination in this country? Yes. Do I identify with the legacy of anti-Jewish sentiment and exclusion? Yes. Do I identify with the internment of Japanese-Americans during World War Two? Yes. Do I identify with the struggle against brutality and genocide waged against the Native Americans in this country? Yes. Do I feel I have to choose one of these allegiances in order to know who I am or in order to pay proper respect to my ancestors? No. Do I hope that what my ancestors love in me is my ability to muster compassion for those who suffer, including myself? Yes. (306–307)

Walker's reflections about compassion and our affinity with all human suffering remind me of a postcard that I have had for many years from the *Syracuse Cultural Workers*. The caption on the card is taken from Pastor Martin Niemoller who led the Church's opposition to Hitler and was imprisoned from 1937 to 1945. His words are well known although sometimes in different versions. It reads:

> First they came for the socialists, and I did not speak out because I was not a socialist.
> Then they came for the trade unionists, and I did not speak out because I was not a trade unionist.
> Then they came for the Jews, and I did not speak out because I was not a Jew.
> Then they came for me, and there was no one left to speak for me.

In his book *When Teachers Face Themselves* (1955), Jersild writes about being compassionate with someone as our being able to enter into the meaning of the feeling that the other person is experiencing.

For example, if someone is angry we do not have to be angry ourselves to be compassionate. Rather, we understand the essence of anger in an emotional way. We do not judge, join with the angry person, or condone the anger. Instead, we draw on our own personal experience or capacity of anger. bell hooks suggests that compassion connects us to others and it comes out of developing the capacity for forgiveness (hooks 2000a). She describes forgiveness as an important component to compassion in that it can heal our wounds.

> Compassion opens the way for individuals to feel empathy for others without judgment. Judging others increases our alienation. When we judge we are less able to forgive. The absence of forgiveness keeps us mired in shame . . . when we practice forgiveness we let go of shame. Embedded in our shame is always a sense of being unworthy. It separates. Compassion and forgiveness reconnect us. (217)

In order to do meaningful anti-bias work teachers must develop compassion to connect with all kinds of children and families—even those that might cause us discomfort. It seems that we can learn to be kind. We are able to develop an affinity for the suffering of others. In that way, we will not stand by and bear witness to oppression of people different from us. We develop compassion when we learn to make peace with our feelings of discomfort.

Having compassion means respecting children's abilities. Anti-bias work and inclusion seem to be especially difficult for early childhood professionals and special education teachers. One of our teachers once called it *intrusion* by mistake. I hear time and again that children with special needs must be able to fit into society. Therefore, teachers do all sorts of interventions to make them fit the mold. Often the methods they use seem to me to be harsh or excessive. When a child is identified with a disability, the dominant culture model immediately comes into play. It seems so difficult to envision a society that could adjust to people with special needs instead of the other way around.

When we try and force someone to fit into a mold we cease to understand what it feels like to walk in his or her shoes. Recently, a few of our teachers were taking their lunch break in my office. Very soon the discussion turned to children. They were trying to understand why the special education therapist was being so hard on one of our toddlers with Down syndrome. The child plays with great intelligence and imagination in the dramatic play area and is progressing at a pace that seems appropriate for him. One of the teachers said with frustration, "Why must this child be like everyone else? It seems to me that the therapist has expectations for him greater than the typical children his age. You would think that she would be more understanding than us regular teachers."

The teachers were referring to the way the therapist forced the child to walk. She would stand him up firmly. As the child dropped to his knees crying and trying to crawl to his caregiver, the therapist would pick him up and stand him back firmly saying, "You can do this." This procedure continued for some time. It was too much for the teacher who finally picked the child up and said to the therapist, "I really think he is trying to tell us he doesn't want to do this." If we want a toddler with Down syndrome to fit into society do we have to force him to walk when he clearly does not want to? In our desperation to fit children into a societal mold do we forget about being compassionate? We forget to try and understand what it feels like to be different.

Compassion means being able to talk honestly with people who have different abilities. For example, our receptionist is paraplegic. One side of her body was paralyzed at age thirteen because of a brain tumor. Sometimes when I am clumsy and drop things she almost yells out loud with laughter. For a while it annoyed me greatly, as it did other staff at the Center. No one felt comfortable enough to talk to her about laughing at my awkwardness. One day I asked her why she laughed when I drop things. She explained that it was a relief for her to see that typical people can be as clumsy as her because she feels clumsy most of the time. It helped her feel included. It was also a relief for her when we started asking her to tell us how she came to be in a wheelchair. Up until then no one talked to her about herself. Now she tells her story to our children and they are able to share in her life experiences as well.

Our discomfort sometimes clouds our compassion. Sometimes we speak loudly to people who do not understand our language or have different abilities. Some people talk loudly or even shout at young children. Perhaps they think young children or people who have different abilities will understand them better if they shout. We ignore people when we fear their difference. When we do that we force them to live in silence. When we have compassion we try and understand what they might be going through even if it is different from our own experience.

Sometimes I wonder if compassion is also just common sense. When I was a preschool teacher in Israel I remember a Canadian family coming to my school. They were concerned about their three-year-old son because he spoke only English. They were worried he would feel uncomfortable because the dominant language was Hebrew. I assured them that I would speak English with him. My assistant teacher was concerned that he would not learn Hebrew if I spoke to him in English. However, he learned Hebrew quicker than we could have imagined. Speaking English to him did not impede his learning. Instead, it made him comfortable and secure and therefore gave him the space to learn a new language. How I wish all children could be treated that way. That would mean that our teachers would need to learn Spanish, Chinese, Korean, Arabic—you name it! I wonder—would that be so bad?

We Become Compassionate When We Confront Our Discomfort

Now as a fifty-three-year-old woman, I look back over my life. I remember with feelings of admiration and love my own mother's courage and compassion as she made a stand for other people's children. I have not always felt that way about her. After all, as I have described in previous chapters, my own childhood was not easy. I felt excluded and unacknowledged. It has taken years of self-reflection and not a little anguish to clear a space for these positive feelings I now describe. I have had to confront my own feelings of rage and loneliness as I worked through to an understanding of my parents and what they were going through when I came into their world. I share this with you because through self-work about my personal experiences and feelings I have been able to transfer what I have learned to my professional life. My work with teachers, students, children, and families has been strengthened, enhanced and, more important, become authentic. The more I understand and accept my uncomfortable feelings, the more compassionate I become.

I wrote a letter in my journal to my mother and father that summed up for me in a few words the experiences I had been going through since my childhood. I did not plan to send the letter to them. My father died in 1981. It was, in fact, a letter that helped me understand what I had learned in my personal struggle along the way. I share it with you as an example of how one might process uncomfortable feelings. Even though my parents were divorced since I was four-years-old, I decided to write to them together. Most children of divorce at some point dream of their parents being together again.

Dear Mom and Dad,

I write to you both together. I have been thinking about you a lot lately. I have been wearing the amethyst ring that you, Dad, gave Mom. At least, that's what she has always told me. I saved it—it had been given to M. I took it back. It's not my style of ring actually, but lately when I wear it I think, "I did have a mother and a father—a mom and a dad—like other people." For so long, since I can remember, I felt that I did not have, did not deserve to have parents like other people. I have been so lonely for so long.

Unbearable loneliness. I watched, all the years as I grew up until recently, and I envied even my own half-siblings. Everyone seemed to have a mother and a father. People, who attend their children's graduations, leave them some inheritance, or support their college education. Indeed, I did all these things for my own son. No one ever came to my graduations. No thought was given for my future. I feel as if I parented myself and adopted surrogate families along the way to take care of me. Dad, I sat alone at your funeral with strangers. Not a word, telegram, or phone call from any member of my family. For years I looked at other people, even my half-siblings, their fathers and mothers visiting and caring, preparing and loving, and I always thought, "Wow, I wish I would be allowed to have parents, real parents."

Lately I think, "Well, actually I did have a Dad and a Mom. Both of them were unprepared emotionally to parent me, though. Each had her/his own problems. Dad was between wives, passing through, old, and couldn't handle it. Mom was overwhelmed, between marriages, in love and insecure, needing to please T. and always terrified of losing him. Wow, what bad timing for me." But, Dad, you gave me a beautiful piano, were proud of me, and treated me gently and with humor. You were so kind to me when we were together. And, Mom, I watched and observed you over the years; your hunger for the arts and your love of books, your ability and strength to help strangers was amazing to see. You always seemed to try and understand your own psyche. That self-reflection and kindness to strangers stayed with me too.

I am going to start to put to rest my longing for a father and mother of my own. I had you both—as dysfunctional and child-like as you both were for me at the time. I have acquired lots of both of your traits: Dad's gentle quality, knowledge of many lan-guages, love of aesthetics and good food, and a love of differ-ences in people. Mom's strength, what strength! You could have made such a contribution to society. Now with both of you in my mind and heart I am working to parent myself and I feel I deserve it. My work with all children makes me know I deserved it. I just came into your lives at a very bad time for you. (My journal entry December 2000)

Facing uncomfortable feelings of loneliness, anger, or jealousy cleared the way for me to see my parents as people with difficulties, frailties, and vulnerabilities of their own. In that way I could allow myself to realize the strengths and characteristics I love and admire about them. As teachers, it is important to realize that this type of self-reflection helps us as we interact with children and families. We be-come able to change our attitudes and assumptions about people different from us. We develop compassion and empathy the more we understand and accept uncomfortable feelings about ourselves.

We Need Courage to Confront Our Discomfort

Confronting our discomfort demands courage. In fact according to Parker J. Palmer, we must have courage to teach at all (1998). In *The Courage to Teach: Exploring the Inner Landscape of a Teacher's Life*, Palmer describes teaching as "a daily exercise in vulnerability" where it is "al-ways done at the dangerous intersection of personal and public life" (17). Further, Palmer claims that good teachers must have *identity* and *integrity*, which "have as much to do with our shadows and limits, our wounds and fears, as with our strengths and potentials" (13). Not wanting us to think of the terms *identity* and *integrity* as "noble fea-tures," Palmer suggests that they are rather "subtle dimensions of the complex, demanding, and lifelong process of self-discovery" (13).

Some of our shadows and limits include feeling fear, which is fundamental to the human condition, according to Palmer. Fear is just one of the many uncomfortable feelings that teachers face. "We cannot see the fear in our students until we see the fear in ourselves. When we deny our own condition, we resist seeing anything in others that might remind us of who, and how *we* really are" (Palmer 1998, 47). When we have the courage to face ourselves, we develop compassion and are then able to take a stand for social justice. "We are able to teach each day in ways that honor [our] deepest values rather than in ways that conform to the institutional norm" or "take risks of a more public sort, promoting alternative visions of education" (171).

One of the fathers of a child in our preschool program was a quiet man who would bring his son into the classroom a little later than the other children each morning. After hugging and kissing his son, he would leave as silently as he came. He hardly ever addressed the teachers even to greet them with the usual "Good morning" that they were expecting. One day he came in later than usual. The time for breakfast was over. However, a few children still sat at the table eating cereal. He made a place for his son to sit when the teacher said sharply, "Breakfast is over." He replied, "But I see children still eating." The teacher took the remaining food and threw it into the garbage bin saying, "It's over." The father took his son and ran out to find help from me. I was out that morning so he found the business manager and complained that his son was hungry and needed breakfast. She took him to the kitchen and gave the child some food.

The next day the teacher and business manager approached me. Each was angry. The teacher was angry with the father for coming late to breakfast and with the business manager's interference in a disciplinary procedure. The business manager was indignant at how the father had been treated. She thought that the teacher should have been kind to him and especially not have excluded his child from breakfast. The teacher went on to explain that this man was aggressive and unfriendly. He never greeted the teachers and was always late bringing in his child in the morning. She thought that it was time to make him understand the classroom schedule.

I knew the man. His son had grown up with us since infancy. Whenever I had observed the father, he was gentle and loving with his child. In my opinion, he seemed to be a shy sort of person. I had never witnessed aggressive behavior from him, and he seemed friendly enough to me, in a reserved fashion. I doubted that he would approach me about the incident and I wanted to hear his side of the story. And so, I put a small note in his child's cubby: "Reminder: Breakfast in the preschool ends at 9:00 A.M." Sure enough, the next day he approached my door carefully. "Can I speak to you a moment?" he said hesitantly. "Of course!" I exclaimed. "Take a seat."

He sat on the edge of the chair in my office and told me how humiliated he had felt when the teacher threw away the cereal in front of him and his child. He could not understand why she had behaved like that nor why she told him breakfast was over when other children were still eating. I mentioned that the teachers were concerned that he always came in late and did not greet them. I wondered, out loud, if the teachers might be afraid of him because he did not talk to them. He explained that he worked night shifts and his wife had to leave very early in the morning. This was the only time he was able to bring his child. He described that, since his childhood, he had suffered exclusion and discrimination and did not really trust people until he knew them well. Therefore, he did not feel comfortable chatting with the teachers when he came to drop off his child in the morning.

I listened carefully and felt grateful that he was able to share with me some of his personal life experiences and vulnerabilities. Again, I wondered out loud. "Do you think the teachers fear you because you are an African American man?" After all, they had not once approached him to talk about what they felt was his tardiness. He laughed heartily and replied wistfully, "Everyone fears African American men." We talked together a bit more about how hard it is to be an African American man when people always fear him. As the father talked, I thought of the young African American poet who had come to my undergraduate class as a guest speaker. I remembered him describing how he heard the locks on car doors of white people snapping shut as he walked by.

I told the father that I would talk to the teacher about it. I asked him if he would allow me to share our discussion with the teacher. He agreed and seemed relieved. I apologized to him for the humiliation and pain he and his child had suffered in the preschool that day. I asked him to try and be friendlier toward the teacher even though he did not know her well. I asked him if he could trust me. He said he would try to be more open with the teacher. He stood up to leave, stopped and looked back at me and said, "Thank you for this talk. I've never talked with a white woman like this before. I can't believe it! This is not what I was expecting to happen in this conversation."

When he left, I invited the preschool teacher into my office to talk about the incident. She listened thoughtfully as I told her the father's story and concerns. Finally I asked her, "Why have you never approached him about coming in late in the mornings?" She shook her head and said that she was afraid to. I asked if she was afraid to approach all the parents that way. She said that she wasn't. "Do you fear him because he is African American?" I asked. She looked uncomfortable for a moment and said in a soft voice that she did. I gently described to her how hard that was for him, and how he felt discriminated against and excluded when she would not allow his child breakfast that morning. I explained how her behavior reinforced for him all the painful experiences he had since his early childhood, and, in fact, caused him to act defensively that morning at breakfast—in the very way she had feared he would react! I suggested that when she felt ready and able to reach out to him she might help him feel more trusting to approach her. She told me that she felt relief at talking about her fear and was grateful for my suggestion to reach out to him.

When the teacher was allowed to share her discomfort safely with me she became able to make space through her fears to feel compassion for the African American father of the child in her classroom. She no longer felt the need to "discipline" him for his tardiness, and understood that he needed us to reach out to him. The next day she sincerely apologized to him. Gradually communication between them improved during the coming months. It is important for administrators and teacher-educators to understand about the discomfort that teachers in their programs might be experiencing. Teachers will be more likely to change their attitudes if they are given support and a safe environment to explore their discomfort.

Built on the ideas of the *Anti-Bias Curriculum: Tools for Empowering Young Children* (Derman-Sparks 1989), *In Our Own Way* is the culmination of teachers' experiences as they take on the challenge of an anti-bias approach in their early childhood programs (Alvarado et al. 1999). Seven teachers tell their stories about how working with an anti-bias approach changed their identities and personal lives. All of them were interviewed in a way that enabled them to explore the challenge of anti-bias work as it became integrated into their lives. The teachers' stories are fascinating in that all of them came to similar conclusions about how anti-bias work was affected by their own early childhood experiences including cultural, direct discrimination or styles of behavior. They all mention how uncomfortable it was to look inside themselves. One of them said:

> As I've been doing this work I've found that most of the resistance I've met has been my own—feeling uncomfortable, feeling like I wasn't ready. There were so many times I would think: God, why did I say or do that? But I would go ahead, and for the most part, it would turn out fine. I'd be glad that I took the chance. (Alvarado et al. 1999, 167)

According to the authors, inequity and prejudice by society and individuals cause great harm to all our children. They write that an anti-bias approach necessitates that teachers engage in constant self-reflection about their assumptions and attitudes. Our early experiences are shaped by participation in the institutions of our society, which are influenced by oppressive systems like sexism and racism. They describe how all seven teachers recall "key childhood experiences that influenced their later commitment to justice," and that "another aspect of self-discovery and change is grappling with one's own discomfort or lack of confidence in speaking out and acting on anti-bias issues" (Alvarado et al. 1999, 184). Furthermore, they conclude that teachers should "open up to feelings of discomfort or uneasiness and investigate what causes them" so that they become "responsible for [their] present and future behavior and attitudes . . . [as] a source of growth" (185).

Every teacher is at a different stage in terms of bias or prejudice. Some are more aware of their biases than others. Some are more confident than others. Over the years, I have learned to have compassion for teachers and realize that they need a safe place to share uncomfortable feelings. The more I give them a secure environment to confront their discomfort, the more understanding they become of children's feelings. Allowing teachers to share unpleasant feelings does not reinforce prejudiced behaviors. Instead, it helps them understand themselves and change their attitudes.

The staff has a joke about me at my center. They say, "If you go to Tamar, you will cry!" In fact, there are many boxes of tissues in my office. I am not afraid if people cry. Confronting our discomfort often causes us to weep. Many women cry when they are angry, for example. Awareness of bias is often accompanied by feelings of guilt and shame. How privileged and grateful I feel when they share some of those intimate feelings with me. On the one hand, they call me the boss, and on the other hand, they come to share with me their most intimate issues of discomfort that arise through teaching young children. As supervisors we can be compassionate in our work with adults.

What Is to Be Done?

For almost a decade, Frances Schoonmaker followed the career growth of one of her student teachers, Kay, from her early years in a teacher preparation program until she became a "teacher lead" (Schoonmaker 2002). The study includes excerpts from Kay's journals as well as feedback from other student teachers about her, and interviews, discussions, and observations by the author. Observing Kay's growth as a teacher, Schoonmaker identifies important implications for teacher preparation in general, and especially as Kay struggles to "reconstruct prior experience in a personally and professionally meaningful way" (44).

In this most recent case study (2002), it is disturbing to read in Schoonmaker's notes that with the exception of Arthur Jersild's work in 1955, teacher preparation programs offer little to no guidance when it comes to the emotional nature of classroom life. "Learning how to deal with the range of emotions that children evoke is one of the challenges of learning to teach. Yet teachers are offered little guidance in learning how to deal with the powerful feelings evoked in classroom life" (Schoonmaker 2002, 59). The author suggests some form of "psychological support" for teachers including collaboration with counseling and psychology departments to explore a "deeper dimension of reflection including the place of emotions in learning to teach" (60). In a number of places throughout the book, Schoonmaker writes with concern about the lack of support and guidance that is given to preservice teachers for self-reflection.

> There are teachers who make a decision to become a teacher because they want to be able to say, "Never again, never again will a child have to suffer what I have suffered." Yet they are given little, if any, support in applying their own experiences to the process of learning about teaching. Learning to teach is also, perhaps even primarily, learning about self. (2002, 43–44)

When we take on the challenge of an anti-bias approach in our classrooms and early childhood programs, we take on the responsibility of confronting our discomfort about how we acquired bias and prejudice. No matter how many good intentions I have, when my subconscious is affecting me I have little control about the decisions I make; nor do I seem able to manage my behaviors in situations that seem to threaten those ingrained survival skills. I have searched for all sorts of ways to support self-reflection, including counseling, journal writing, inspirational posters, bibliotherapy, and by acquiring a higher education. It has not been easy. I continue to work at self-understanding in all these different ways. I still have a lot to do and probably always will.

Reaching out for support does not come easily for everyone. Most teachers go out into the early childhood field unprepared to deal with children's emotions. They have little knowledge or understanding about the diverse populations of parents and guardians they will encounter in their work. They probably have not received much training or practice about understanding their inner, emotional life. Most teacher preparation programs neglect this aspect of education. Once teachers reach their classrooms they are on their own. Hours, days, weeks, months, and years go by and they are left unchallenged about their biases. In many early childhood programs, teachers are judged and made accountable by their competence in classroom management and creating plans or progress reports. No one reviews their self-reflection ability.

I remember a teacher who rushed into my office in shock because one of the children said that all the black children in the class smelled bad. She could not believe that children could say such things. She was at a loss about what to do. She wept with fear. I suggested she talk to the parents of the child but she was afraid to talk about such things. We talked about her fear of unpleasant situations and confrontation in general. She had grown up learning to avoid or deny what she termed "bad feelings." After she shared her discomfort with me, she was able to talk to the parents. She discovered that the child's parents were as upset as she was to hear about racist comments from their child. The next day, the teacher, parents, and all the children in the class had circle time together where they talked about differences in people, smells, and hurtful language. They talked about the only rule we have in our center: "We want everyone to be safe here." That means safety for everyone: teachers, children, and families—in every way, physically and emotionally.

Another time we invited an African American couple to talk to us about their child's progress. Having been born prematurely, their two-year-old was severely delayed and received early intervention services at the center. The four special education teachers and therapists, as well as two teachers from the center and I arranged to talk to the couple about their child's development. When the couple arrived they were given two chairs that faced a semicircle of all seven of us—teachers and therapists. We were all white women. For what seemed like a long moment, everyone sat in uncomfortable silence. No one knew where to begin.

The discomfort became too much for me. I blurted out forthrightly, "How does it feel to be African Americans faced with a wall of white women who all think they are experts about your child?" The couple giggled. I could hear the teachers and therapists shifting uneasily in their seats. The father said, "Quite uncomfortable actually." I asked, "How would you like us to change the seating arrangement?" He replied, "I want you to sit next to me." I moved my chair over to where he was sitting. One of the therapists moved closer to the mother. Almost immediately, there was a release of tension in the room, and this time the mother started the discussion by talking about their child's progress.

At the end of the session, the teachers and therapists summed up the discussion. One of the teachers expressed her dismay about when I had asked the couple how they felt about "white versus black" as she termed it. However, she was relieved to see that it had helped create a more open and safe environment for them all to communicate. She expressed her surprise that the father had invited me to sit next to him. She said, "How would we have known he felt that way unless we asked him?" Not only did we talk about white versus black, but we also addressed the issue of parents versus the experts. By speaking it out loud we were able to break down the barriers of the us versus them and become equal partners in the care and education of this young child.

Many teachers are like me and find their own way for self-reflection. I fear that many more do not, and are left alone without any support at all. I dreamed of participating in a support group when I was a teacher alone in my classroom. As discussed in Chapter 5, I was privileged to facilitate one in 1995. The group participants learned a lot about themselves and started to make connections between their early memories and professional lives that helped change their attitudes. Such support groups would help teachers with this important aspect of their teaching. They could be ongoing, organized groups small enough to encourage intimate discussion, and facilitated by a person with counseling skills as well as knowledge of teaching. However, the group's purpose should not become a venting and complaining session. It is crucial that the facilitator helps teachers focus on specifically making connections between their own learned biases and, consequently, interactions with children and families. It is those kinds of connections that help teachers make intentional, conscious decisions that break down the barriers that are caused by our biases.

A support-supervision group is an excellent setting for early childhood professionals who are challenged with issues of low self-esteem. When a teacher feels victimized or marginalized, she tends not to believe that she deserves respect, or is able to acquire a higher education. These are difficult feelings to overcome without support. In a support group, we gather strength from each other. We realize that others have similar fears to us and together we learn to overcome them. As a group, we share different ways of dealing with feelings, life experiences, and are not left alone as we try to create new solutions together.

I have another dream. I wish that communities would band together and decide that this type of support is fundamental for teaching for social justice; and that top government officials and administrators would invest large sums of money to facilitate this type of pre-service and in-service teacher development. I wish everyone would view it to be as important as literacy, mathematics, or technology. The early childhood teaching community has come a long way in endorsing our anti-bias work. However, we have only begun to scratch the surface in addressing the terrible harm done to children by prejudice, inequity, and bias. We continue to be blocked by shame, fear, guilt, or old useless survival skills. Confronting our discomfort is one of the keys to clear the way for an anti-bias approach. There is so much emotion at so many levels for teachers to deal with in the early childhood profession. We simply cannot do it all on our own!

Final Thoughts

There are great rewards in having the courage to confront our discomfort and develop compassion. We become more conscious of the decisions we make as we interact with children or teachers in our classrooms and programs. We feel connected and are able to make a difference in a meaningful way to children and families. Compassion is crucial as we do anti-bias work in early childhood programs. It gives us the space to hear other people's stories. We begin to let down our guard, develop more useful and friendly survival skills, and become more accepting of and less threatened by differences. The less frightened we are, the more we can let go of our anger and resentment. We become more confident personally and professionally.

Letting go of old survival skills can be frightening and painful. Many of us need support to do this work. Some use journal writing, formal education, or counseling. Others become aware of bias through reading, watching movies, or learning from different stories and biographies. I like to surround myself with inspirational posters. I recommend forming support-supervision groups to make it less lonely as we struggle to confront our discomfort. In these kinds of groups, it is important to have a professional facilitator to help us focus specifically on the connections we make between our biases and the work that we do. The political is personal, and the personal affects our professional work. It is all connected. The challenge, and fun of it, is discovering where they all intertwine and, thus, influence us.

We might choose to let go of some of our biases, and we might have to keep some with us. It takes time to delve into our own early childhood experiences we discover feelings of hurt, anger, fear and guilt. As we explore our shadows and limitations—our prejudices, our bias—we develop an affinity with all beings who suffer. Compassion enriches and enhances our understanding of the human condition. We become activists, more and more able to do powerful anti-bias work, and less afraid to stand up for what is right.

I have an intellectual family that resides inside my mind. Lilian Katz is one of them. I have chosen its members to be all the people who have ever inspired me to think about and understand why I do what I do in my work with children and families. Their words strengthen and remind me of my awesome responsibility as an educator, because how I interact with children matters—it affects them for the rest of their lives. I share with you the conclusion of Katz's *Last Class Notes* from the symposium held in her honor in November 2000:

> I really believe that each of us must come to care about everyone else's children. We must come to see that the well-being of our own individual children is intimately linked to the well-being of all other people's children. After all, when one of our own children needs life-saving surgery, someone else's child will perform it; when one of our own children is threatened or harmed by violence on the streets, someone else's child will commit it. The good life for our own children can only be secured if it is also secured for all people's children. But to worry about all other people's children is not just a practical or strategic matter; it is a moral and ethical one: to strive for the well-being of all other people's children *is also right*.
>
> Remember that whoever might be president of our country in forty or fifty years is likely to be in someone's early childhood program today; and I hope she is having a good experience! (Katz 2000, 394)

References

Accreditation Criteria and Procedures of the National Academy of Early Childhood Programs. 1998. A publication of the National Association for the Education of Young Children.

Alvarado, C., L. Burnley, L. Derman-Sparks et al. 1999. *In Our Own Way: How Anti-Bias Work Shapes Our Lives.* St. Paul, MN: Redleaf Press.

Ayers, W. 1989. *The Good Preschool Teacher.* New York: Teachers College Press.

———. 1991. "Teaching and Being." In *Critical Perspectives on Early Childhood Education,* L. Weis, P. G. Altbach, G. P. Kelly, and H. G. Petrie, eds. Albany, NY: State University of New York Press.

———. Conversation with author. November 13, 1992.

———. 1993. *To Teach: The Journey of a Teacher.* New York: Teachers College Press.

———. 1998. Foreword. *Teaching for Social Justice,* W. Ayers, J. A. Hunt, and T. Quinn, eds. New York: The New Press and Teachers College Press.

Banks, J. A. (1993). Multicultural education for young children: Racial and ethnic attitudes and their modification. In B. Spodek (ed.), *A Handbook of Research on the Education of Young Children,* 236–251. New York: Macmillan Publishing Company.

Bowman, B. T. 1989. "Self Reflection as an Element of Professionalism." *Teacher College Record* 90 (3): 444–51.

Bredekamp, S., and S. Glowacki. 1996. The first decade of NAEYC accreditation: Growth and impact on the field. In S. Bredekamp and B. A. Willer, eds., *NAEYC Accreditation: A Decade of Learning and the Years Ahead.* Washington, DC: National Association for the Education of Young Children.

Brown, S. I. 1982. "On Humanistic Alternatives in the Practice of Teacher Education." *Journal of Research and Development in Education* 15 (4): 1–12.

Carter, P. A. 2002. *"Everybody's Paid But the Teacher": The Teaching Profession and the Women's Movement.* New York: Teachers College Press.

Caruso, J. S., and M. T. Fawcett. 1986. *Supervision in Early Childhood*

Education: A Developmental Perspective. New York: Teachers College Press.

Chesler, P. 2001. *Woman's Inhumanity to Woman*. New York: Thunder's Mouth Press/Nation Books.

Clandinin, D. J., A. Davies, P. Hogan, and B. Kennard. 1993. *Learning to Teach, Teaching to Learn: Stories of Collaboration in Teacher Education*. New York: Teachers College Press.

Clinebell, C. H. 1973. *Meet Me in the Middle: On Becoming Human Together*. New York: Harper & Row.

Combs, A. W. 1965. *The Professional Education of Teachers: A Perceptual View of Teacher Preparation*. Boston: Allyn & Bacon.

Cronin, S., L. Derman-Sparks, S. Henry, C. Olatunji, and S. York. 1998. *Future Vision Present Work: Learning from the Culturally Relevant Anti-Bias Leadership Project*. St. Paul, MN: Redleaf Press.

Debold, E., M. Wilson, and I. Malave. 1993. *Mother Daughter Revolution: From Betrayal to Power*. Boston: Addison-Wesley.

Delpit, L. 1995. *Other People's Children: Cultural Conflict in the Classroom*. New York: The New Press.

Derman-Sparks, L. 1989. *Anti-Bias Curriculum: Tools for Empowering Young Children*. Washington, DC: National Association for the Education of Young Children.

———. 1998. "Educating for Equality: Forging a Shared Vision." In *Beyond Heroes and Holidays: A Practical Guide to K–12 Anti-Racist, Multicultural Education and Staff Development*, E. Lee, D. Menkart, and M. Okazawa-Rey, eds. Washington, DC: Network of Educators on the Americas.

Dewey, J. 1933. *How We Think: A Restatement of the Relation of Reflective Thinking to the Educative Process*. Boston: D. C. Heath.

Dove, R. 1999. *On the Bus with Rosa Parks: Poems*. New York: W. W. Norton.

Edelman, M. W. 1993. *The Measure of Our Success: A Letter to My Children and Yours*. New York: HarperPerennial.

———. 1999. *Lanterns: A Memoir of Mentors*. Boston: Beacon Press.

Espinosa, L. M. 1997. "Personal Dimensions of Leadership." In *Leadership in Early Care and Education*, S. L. Kagan and B. T. Bowman, eds. Washington, DC: National Association for the Education of Young Children.

Fenichel, E. 1992. *Learning Through Supervision and Mentorship to Support the Development of Infants, Toddlers, and Their Families: A Source Book*. Zero to 3. Arlington, VA: National Center for Clinical Infant Programs.

Fu, V. R., A. J. Stremmel., and C. Treppte. 1993. *Multiculturalism in*

Early Childhood Programs. Urbana, IL: Perspectives from ERIC/EECE: A Monograph Series, No. 3. ERIC Clearinghouse on Elementary Early Childhood Education.

Gadamer, H. G. 1976. *Philosophical Hermeneutics*. Berkley: University of California Press.

Garbarino, J. Conversation with author. May 29, 1997.

Garcia, E. E., and B. McLaughlin. 1995. Introduction. In E. E. Garcia and B. McLaughlin, with Spodek and Saracho, eds., *Yearbook in Early Childhood Education, vol. 6*, viii–ix. New York: Teachers College Press.

Geras, N. 1999. *The Contract of Mutual Indifference: Political Philosophy After the Holocaust*. London: Verso.

Goleman, D. 1997. *Emotional Intelligence: Why It Can Matter More Than IQ*. New York: Bantam.

Gonzalez-Mena, J. 1993. *Multicultural Issues in Child Care*. Mountain View, CA: Mayfield.

Goodson, I. F. 1992. *Studying Teachers' Lives*. New York: Teachers College Press.

Gordon, A., and K. W. Browne. 1996. *Guiding Young Children in a Diverse Society*. Boston: Allyn & Bacon.

Greenberg, H. M. 1969. *Teaching with Feeling: Compassion and Awareness in the Classroom Today*. New York: Macmillan.

Greenberg-Lake (The Analysis Group). 1994. *Shortchanging Girls, Shortchanging America: Executive Summary*. Washington, DC: American Association of University Women.

Greene, B. 2002. *Get with the Program! Getting Real About Your Health, Weight, and Emotional Well-Being*. New York: Simon & Schuster.

Greer, G. 1999. *The Whole Woman*. London: Doubleday.

Hall, I., C. H. Campbell, and E. J. Miech. 1997. *Class Acts: Teachers Reflect on Their Own Classroom Practice*. Cambridge, MA: Harvard Education.

Harris, J. H. 1906. "Everybody's Paid by the Teacher." The Women's Journal (February 3) 37: 20.

Holland, D. C., and M. A. Eisenhart. 1990. *Educated in Romance: Women, Achievement, and College Culture*. Chicago: University of Chicago Press.

hooks, b. 2000a. *All About Love: New Visions*. Cambridge, MA: South End Press.

———. 2000b. *Feminism Is for Everybody: Passionate Politics*. Cambridge, MA: South End Press.

Jacobson, T. 1999. "What We Do Matters." *Child Care Information Exchange* (November/December) (130): 60–62.

―――. 2000. "Prod and Pry from Inside Out: An Ethnography of an Anti-bias Support-Supervision Group for Teachers of Young Children." In Proceedings of Lilian Katz Symposium: *Issues in Early Childhood Education: Curriculum, Teacher Education, and the Dissemination of Information.* November 6, ERIC Clearinghouse, University of Illinois at Urbana Champagne.

Jersild, A. T. 1954. "Understanding Others Through Facing Ourselves." *Childhood Education* (May): 411–14.

―――. 1955. *When Teachers Face Themselves.* New York: Teachers College Press.

Jones, E. 1993. *Growing Teachers: Partnerships in Staff Development.* Washington, DC: National Association for the Education of Young Children.

Kagan, S. L. 1998. "Professional Development/Quality Improvement in the Field of Early Childhood Education." Paper presented at Erie County Legislative Breakfast, Buffalo, New York, February 13.

Kapuscinski, R. 1985. "Reflections Revolution II the Dead Flame." Translated from the Polish by William R. Brand and Kataszyna Mcoczkowska-Brand. *The New Yorker* (March 11): 89 and 90.

Karr-Morse, R., and M. S. Wiley. 1997. *Ghosts from the Nursery: Tracing the Roots of Violence.* New York: Atlantic Monthly Press.

Katz, L. G. 1993. "The National Goals Wish List: Message from the President." *Young Children* (February): 3.

―――. 2000. "Last Class Notes." Proceedings of Lilian Katz Symposium: *Issues in Early Childhood Education: Curriculum, Teacher Education, and the Dissemination of Information.* November 7, ERIC Clearinghouse, University of Illinois at Urbana Champagne.

Kendall, F. 1983. *Diversity in the Classroom: A Multicultural Approach to the Education of Young Children.* New York: Teachers College Press.

Kenyatta, M., and R. H. Tai, eds. 1997. Foreword. Symposium on Ethnicity and Education. *Harvard Education Review* 67 (2): vii–ix.

Kozol, J. 1991. *Savage Inequalities: Children in America's Schools.* New York: Crown.

Lawrence, S. M., and B. D. Tatum. 1998. "White racial identity and anti-racist education: A catalyst for change." In *Beyond Heroes and Holidays: A Practical Guide to K–12 Anti-Racist, Multicultural Education and Staff Development,* E. Lee, D. Menkart, and M. Okazawa-Rey, eds. Washington, DC: Network of Educators on the Americas.

Levine, M. 1988. "An Analysis of Mutual Assistance." *American Journal of Community Psychology* 6 (2): 167–88.

Mamet, D. 2001. "A Beloved Friend Who Lived Life the Chicago Way." *The New York Times,* 14 October, p. 7.

McCracken, J. B. 1993. *Valuing Diversity: The Primary Years*. Washington, DC: National Association for the Education of Young Children.

McIntosh, P. 1988. "White Privilege: Unpacking the Invisible Knapsack." In *White Privilege and Male Privilege: A Personal Account of Coming to See Correspondences Through Work in Women's Studies*. Essay excerpted from Working Paper 189. Wellesley College for Center for Research on Women, Wellesley, MA 02181.

Meyer, T. 1997. "Anti-Bias Support-Supervision Group for Early Educators: An Ethnographic Investigation." Unpublished doctoral dissertation, State University of New York at Buffalo.

———. 1998. "In and Out of Confidence." *AEYC of WNY Newsletter*, November/December.

Miller, A. 2001. *The Truth Will Set You Free: Overcoming Emotional Blindness and Finding Your True Adult Self*. New York: Basic Books.

Moore, M. 2001. *Stupid White Men: And Other Sorry Excuses for the State of the Nation*. New York: HarperCollins.

National Association for the Education of Young Children. 1994. "NAEYC Position Statement: A Conceptual Framework for Early Childhood Professional Development." *Young Children* 49 (3): 68–77.

———. 1995. "Understanding Quality and the Cultural Context." *The Academy Update: Early Childhood Professionals Collaborating for Quality* 10 (Fall): 1, 6–7.

Neugebauer, B. 1992. *Alike and Different: Exploring Our Humanity with Young Children*. Washington, DC: National Association for the Education of Young Children.

Nieto, S. 1998. "Affirmation, Solidarity and Critique: Moving Beyond Tolerance in Education." In *Beyond Heroes and Holidays: A Practical Guide to K–12 Anti-Racist, Multicultural Education and Staff Development*, E. Lee, D. Menkart, and M. Okazawa-Rey, eds. Washington, DC: Network of Educators on the Americas.

Olmos, E. J. 2002. "We Are All in the Same World." Keynote address at the California State Association for the Education of Young Children Conference, Long Beach, California, March 2.

Olmos, E. J., L. Ybarra, and M. Monterrey. 1999. *Americanos: Latino Life in the United States*. New York: Little, Brown.

Palmer, P. J. 1998. *The Courage to Teach: Exploring the Inner Landscape of a Teacher's Life*. San Francisco: Jossey-Bass.

Partridge, N. 1972. *Not Alone: A Story for the Future of Rhodesia*. London: SCM Press Ltd.

Perry, B. 2001. "The Core Strengths of a Healthy Child: How Promoting Emotional and Social Well-Being Prevents Violence." Lecture at annual conference of the National Association for the Education of Young Children, Anaheim, California, October 31.

———. 2002. "Nature and Nurture of Brain Development: How Early Experience Shapes Child and Culture." Lecture at annual conference of the Association for the Education of Young Children of Western New York, Buffalo, New York, October 11.

Person, E. S. 2002. *Feeling Strong: The Achievement of Authentic Power*. New York: HarperCollins.

Ramsey, P. G. 1998. *Teaching and Learning in a Diverse World: Multicultural Education for Young Children*. New York: Teachers College Press.

Rich, S. J. 1991. "The Spontaneously-Developed Teacher Support Group: Generation, Evolution and Implication for Professional Development." Unpublished doctoral dissertation, University of Toronto, Canada.

Richardson, V. 1990. "Significant and Worthwhile Change in Teaching Practice." *Educational Researcher* 19 (7): 10–18.

Robinson, A., and D. S. Stark. 2002. *Advocates in Action: Making a Difference for Young Children*. Washington, DC: National Association for the Education of Young Children.

Schoonmaker, F. 2002. *"Growing Up" Teaching: From Personal Knowledge to Professional Practice*. New York: Teachers College Press.

Shapon-Shevin, M. 1999. *Because We Can Change the World*. Boston: Allyn & Bacon.

Silverstein, S. 1964. *The Giving Tree*. New York: HarperCollins.

Steinem, G. 1993. *Revolution from Within: A Book of Self-Esteem*. Boston: Little, Brown.

Vernon-Jones, R. 1993. "Combating Racism Through Support Listening." Paper presented at 48th Annual Conference of Association for Supervision and Curriculum Development, Washington, DC, March 27–30.

Vold, E. B. 1992. *Multicultural Education in Early Childhood Classrooms*. A National Education Association Publication.

Walker, R. 2001. *Black White and Jewish: Autobiography of a Shifting Self*. New York: Riverhead Books.

Walters, M., B. Carter, P. Papp, and O. Silverstein. 1988. *The Invisible Web: Gender Patterns in Family Relationships*. New York: Guilford Press.

Washington, V., and J. D. Andrews. 1998. *Children of 2010*. Washington, DC: National Association for the Education of Young Children.

Wellhousen, K. 1996. "Do's and Don'ts for Eliminating Hidden Bias." *Childhood Education* 73 (1): 36–39.

Wolf, N. 1997. *Promiscuities: The Secret Struggle for Womanhood.* New York: Random House.

Woolford, M. 2002. "America." Poem read at a peace rally in Buffalo, New York, October 6.

Yonemura, M. V. 1986. *A Teacher at Work: Professional Development and the Early Childhood Educator.* New York: Teachers College Press.

York, S. 1991. *Roots and Wings: Affirming Culture in Early Childhood Programs.* St. Paul, MN: Redleaf Press.